AN INTRODUCTION TO PROPERTY VALUATION
VALUATION
(Third Edition)

AN INTRODUCTION TO PROPERTY VALUATION

(Third Edition)

by

A. F. MILLINGTON

B.Sc. (Estate Management), F.R.I.C.S., F.R.V.A., F.B.I.M.

Dean of the Faculty of Business and Land Economy
Hawkesbury College, New South Wales.
One time Professor of Land Economics at Paisley College
One-time Lecturer in Valuation at Reading University; one-time Lecturer in
Valuation at the College of Estate Management

1988

THE ESTATES GAZETTE LIMITED
151 WARDOUR STREET, LONDON W1V 4BN

FIRST PUBLISHED 1975
SECOND IMPRESSION 1976
REPRINTED WITH AMENDMENTS 1979
SECOND EDITION 1982
SECOND IMPRESSION 1984
THIRD IMPRESSION 1986
THIRD EDITION 1988
SECOND IMPRESSION 1989

ISBN 0 7282 0116 X

Printed in Great Britain at The Bath Press, Avon

CONTENTS

cash flow, net present value method and the "target rate", valuation using net present value method, general comments on net present value method, the internal rate of return, a comparison of the net present value and internal rate of return methods, general.

PREFACE TO
FIRST EDITION

Writing this book has only been made possible as a result of the help of many people, and I would like to express my thanks to the following:

My wife and family for tolerating their neglect whilst I was writing the book and for encouraging me to write it:

My mother for encouraging and assisting me to enter the profession of the land:

My teachers during my education at the College of Estate Management, in particular my past tutor, past colleague, and friend Mr. Tony Johnson without whose prodding and encouragement I should probably never have put pen to paper:

My past employers and colleagues at Edwards, Bigwood and Bewlay of Birmingham for the help and experience I gained whilst with them:

Mr. F. P. Wilson and the staff of the Estates Gazette for their assistance and for producing this book:

Mrs. Linda Pullen who with great patience did the majority of the typing:

My colleagues at Reading University and my friends in the profession for the accumulated knowledge and ideas obtained from them.

A. F. Millington
July, 1975

PREFACE TO
SECOND EDITION

The original objectives of the book have been retained in this edition. The opportunity has been taken to up-date material where necessary for many changes in detail have occurred in the space of a few years. Additionally, discussion of certain topics has been expanded in the light of their greater relevance with the passage of time, whilst certain new material has been added. In particular a new chapter giving an introduction to discounted cash flow has been added as, even in an introductory book, it is no longer appropriate to leave this topic to later stages of study.

In addition to those mentioned in the preface to the first edition the author is grateful for the invaluable assistance given by Mr. Roger Emeny, lecturer in valuation at Reading University, and Mr. Will Fraser, lecturer in valuation at Paisley College, in respect of the new chapter on discounted cash flow techniques.

Alan Millington
August 1981

PREFACE TO
THIRD EDITION

The general objectives in this edition have been to keep to the same basic approach as in earlier editions, but to up-date the content to take account of ever-changing conditions in the world, and in the property world in particular.

Whereas in years past financial and property markets operated on national scales, there is no doubt whatsoever that today there are world markets in finance and property investment. International property investment is a major and expanding business, and the book has been adapted to make it more easily understandable to international readers by the inclusion of expressions used in countries other than Britain. I am indebted to Mr. David Lloyd, lecturer in Valuation and Real Estate at Hawkesbury College, New South Wales, Australia, for his assistance in relating Australian and American terminology to that normally used in Britain.

For readers whose currency is not the pound sterling it should be noted that all references in the mathematics of valuation to the Present Value of £1, the Amount of £1 etc., can be altered to the Present Value of $1 etc. or any other unit of currency without in any way altering the validity of the concepts or the functioning of the multiplier concerned.

Other matters of updating include the addition of observations on the unitisation of property interests, and the further development of concepts introduced in earlier editions of the book.

A. F. Millington
November, 1987

CHAPTER 1

INTRODUCTION

The purpose of this book is to provide general background reading for students of surveying, estate management and land economics, who have not previously studied valuation. The lack of such a book was first noted by the author when he was a student, and the need became more apparent to him whilst he was a lecturer in valuation at the College of Estate Management and the University of Reading.

The book is written principally for students studying for the examinations of the professional bodies connected with the land (such as the Royal Institution of Chartered Surveyors and the Incorporated Society of Valuers and Auctioneers), and those studying for degrees in Estate Management and related subject areas. It is also hoped that it may prove of interest to students in other disciplines, including possibly economics and banking, and the author would be more than a little flattered if it proved to be of interest to any qualified practitioners.

No book can hope to be a completely authoritative work on any subject, and this does not even attempt to be that. It is hoped that it will be used primarily for background reading, and there will inevitably be gaps in it where it does not cover a specific examination syllabus. It is not intended to do that, but meant to be used as a basic primer. More detailed and intensive studies of many of the topics should be obtained from more advanced text-books such as "Modern Methods of Valuation" published by The Estates Gazette, London.

The author hopes it will prove to be the sort of book that can be read in bed or in the bath, and, although he would like to think that much of it will be remembered it is not intended to be read and learnt "parrot-fashion".

If, having read it, a student has acquired a good background to valuation and a general understanding of the basic principles of the subject, the author will feel his efforts have been worthwhile. He does not profess or attempt to "answer all the questions". If, on reaching the end of the book the reader feels that there are many questions unanswered he offers no apologies, but on the contrary will be pleased, as it will suggest that interest has been aroused and the appetite whetted for further study of a fascinating subject.

Every effort has been made to ensure that errors have been eliminated, and apologies are given for any that may have crept through.

The book is in no way intended to be taken as giving professional advice on specific matters, and neither the author nor anyone connected with its publication can accept responsibility for the results of any action taken, or any advice given, as a result of reading it. Indeed, if it teaches nothing more than that there are no hard and fast rules that can be applied in property investment and general investment, and that there are rarely, if ever, two identical situations in property and the property world, the book will have taught something useful.

For the benefit of those with a legal grounding, it must be mentioned that as the chief purpose of this book is to discuss the valuation of real property and leasehold property, the word "property" is used throughout these pages in a somewhat loose way to refer to these items, to the exclusion of items of personal property other than leaseholds.

CHAPTER 2

GENERAL

The ownership of property is a form of holding money and thus when we consider the valuation of property we are concerned with money. It is therefore essential for the newcomer to valuation to get to know the way investors think. Both the student and the experienced practitioner should understand what is happening in the world of finance generally, and with this in mind the financial pages of a good newspaper should be read regularly. The more you know about the way monied people and institutions think and act, the better equipped you will be to become a skilled valuer. What are people currently spending their money on? What is the trend? What changes in investment policy are taking place? What is being done with money? Why are these things happening? These are all critical questions for the professional adviser to ask.

For property matters in particular it is necessary to become a regular reader of "Estates Gazette", which is the magazine of the United Kingdom property world, being published weekly. Similar journals are published in other countries with active property markets and should be read as appropriate. Initially, much of the contents may mean little to the new reader, but with regular reading he will soon find that he is getting the feel of the property world, and within a short time a good understanding of activities in the market will be obtained. He should not try to learn the contents but should read it as he would read any other magazine, paying more attention to the items he finds particularly interesting, because in this way he will find the branch of the property world which interests him most, and this will be a great help if at a later stage a specialisation has to be chosen.

Indeed, it is probably timely at this stage to emphasise that it is wrong to try to "learn" a subject such as valuation. Concentration should be directed towards trying to understand articles which are read and topics which are discussed. Learning without understanding is pointless. If there is understanding, learning will tend to follow automatically, and, even more important, opinions will be formed which will enable topics to be discussed. Moreover, a subject which is understood will almost inevitably be more interesting than one which is not understood.

The approach in this book will be to look very generally at property and valuations on the assumption that the reader has no knowledge of the subject and is in very much the same position as a person who is learning a new language. Some of the chapters will be almost entirely mathematical in content, but the reader with a non-mathematical mind should not put the book down at this stage, nor should he avoid the particular chapters concerned. The mathematical content is very basic indeed, and no-one need have any fears about not being able to understand it.

Valuation is not simply a mathematical process. It is much more than that, and probably the larger part of the valuation process depends upon the valuer forming opinions. He has to look at a wide range of facts and he has to try to predict the future. He almost has to become a crystal-gazer. He has to weigh up all the facts in a particular situation, and, having done so, then form opinions upon which his valuation will be based.

There are probably many definitions of "valuation". It can be defined as "The art, or science, of estimating the value for a specific purpose of a particular interest in property at a particular moment in time, taking into account all the features of the property and also considering all the underlying economic factors of the market, including the range of alternative investments". There will be different definitions, and the student will note that this definition itself is somewhat all-embracing and vague, even though it is long.

It is sometimes said that valuation is an art, and sometimes that it is a science. In fact it is a mixture of both, and in some instances the scientific content will be the greater, whilst in others the process will be almost entirely an art. The scientific part of valuations is the analysis of data and the mathematical calculations of value; the art is the skill of knowing which information to use to assist one's valuation, and the process of making judgements and forming opinions. Whatever it is called, valuation is not a simple cut-and-dried process, and although it may appear so when an experienced valuer is at work this is only because he has previously gone through all the processes of training and is now so familiar with the job that it appears simple and rapid.

In most instances the mathematical content of a valuation will be very simple. Valuation could also be defined as "The art of expressing opinions in a mathematical form in order to arrive at the value of a particular interest in a particular piece of property at a given moment of time". It is getting to the stage of being able to put opinions into a mathematical form which presents the problems—searching for all the facts concerning the property interest and the area in which it is situated, considering all these facts, and subsequently forming opinions.

In order to study the background to valuation, it will help to consider the first definition at some length.

The definition mentions the range of alternative investments, and this is all-important. The ownership of property is a form of holding money, and it is necessary to consider what people who have money do with it. All the items on which it could be spent should be considered. Money is not normally spent without the alternatives open to the spender being considered. There will always be the spendthrift who confounds this theory, but, generally speaking, money is only spent after careful thought, the more so in the case of large amounts. People wish to get value for money, and the valuer will endeavour to advise a potential purchaser of a figure which will ensure that this happens. A property which is purchased should be a good investment to the buyer or he would be better advised to spend his money elsewhere on something which gives him better value for money.

People who have money can always simply spend it on what could be termed instant enjoyment. An expensive and rapid sports car could be bought, visits could be made to night clubs and popular places of entertainment, an expensive wardrobe could be bought and meals be enjoyed at the best restaurants. Expensive and luxurious holidays could be taken and the spender could generally "live it up". And what is wrong with that? Although personally we may disapprove of such action, who are we to say that another should not spend money in such a way? If the person concerned gets the greatest satisfaction from such expenditure then it is difficult to say that it is unwise, although it may well be that in later years, if he lives long enough, the spender will have formed different opinions and will have different needs, which may cause him to regret his earlier excessive expenditure on instant pleasure. Nevertheless, when considering the options open to an investor, it should always be borne in mind that any expenditure on investment should give the spender at least equal value to expenditure on his immediate needs and requirements.

It is possible to spend money on more durable consumer goods such as articles for the home, the home itself, tools of a trade, or possibly on the education of children. All expenditure of this type gives longer-lasting returns than does expenditure on "instant pleasure". The returns come principally in the form of the use given by the articles, but there may be an eventual money return of a somewhat remote form, in that the home and the articles in it have a very definite effect on the well-being of the occupiers and on their ability to work efficiently in their jobs, whilst tools of a trade and education assist in earning a living. So we see that when money is spent in this way returns come over a longer period of time than with expenditure on pleasure, and there may even be indirect financial returns.

There is a wide range of investments in which money can be placed such as stocks and shares, National Savings Certificates, gilt-edged securities, debentures, Local Authority Loans, Building Society shares and deposit accounts, assurance and endowment policies, unit trusts, investment trusts, property bonds, or, if a person is interested in landed property, either shares in property companies or investment directly in property itself. Of a more material nature than many of these items, but probably requiring smaller capital funds than landed property, there are investments such as silver, antique furniture, porcelain, works of art and the like.

With such a wide range of investment opportunities, the alternatives open to the investor should be studied before he ties up money in bricks and mortar. Unless such a study is made, how can he really be sure that he is making the right decision if he purchases a property interest? Some of these outlets for money will later be considered at greater length.

CHAPTER 3

QUALITIES OF INVESTMENTS

The potential investor's final choice should logically be that investment with features which make it nearest to his ideal investment. Different investments will vary considerably in their features and it is necessary to consider those which might appeal to different investors.

It is possible to list many qualities, but there are some which will be more important than others and which will be regular considerations for most investors. These will include security of capital, liquidity of capital, the security of income, the regularity of income, the ease of purchase and sale, the costs of purchase and sale, the divisibility of holdings, the security in real terms, and capital appreciation prospects.

Security of capital is a most important feature, because few investors will want to place their money in an investment if the prospect of losing that money is high. Only the gambler, or the person who has so much money that he is able to risk losing some, will be prepared to put his money into a risky venture and, even then, only if there is some possibility of a large gain if all goes well. The vast majority of investors will only wish to place their money in an investment if there is a strong probability that they will be able to recoup their capital at any point in time should the need arise. The greater the chances of their being able to get their original money back at any point in time (or the greater the security of their capital), the greater will be their willingness to invest. If the chance of getting the original money back is slight, then an investment will be considered insecure and relatively unattractive.

Security of income is another important consideration, and it must be remembered that, in investing his money, an investor is giving up the immediate use of that money and is allowing its use to pass to some other party. If a person gave up the use of any other article which he owned, such as a car, he would expect the lender to pay a hire fee, and it is just the same with the investor. In return for giving the use of his money to someone else, he requires payment, and this payment will be the interest his money earns. It is his reward for forgoing the use of his own money, and before he is prepared to give it up he will wish to be reasonably certain that he will get adequate payment for such use, and that there is a high degree of certainty that the payment will in fact be made.

Coupled with the certainty that adequate interest will be paid, will also be the wish in most instances to receive *regular payments of interest*. If regular payments are made the borrower is less likely to get into arrears, whilst the receipt of interest at regular intervals enables the lender to phase such receipts to meet regular expenditure which he may be incurring, and this will assist his own budgetary control.

Investments which are *easy to purchase and sell* will be particularly attractive to an investor who may be likely to require his capital at relatively short notice. If such a need is likely to arise it would be foolish to place money in investments on which notice has to be given before repayment of the capital will be made, unless such notice is very short indeed. Frequently, where notice is required it is in terms of months rather than days, and an investor will be at a considerable disadvantage if, having placed his money in an investment which requires two to three months' notice before withdrawal of capital can be made, he suddenly has to meet unexpected debts within a matter of days. If such a situation is likely to arise he will be better off if his money is invested in something from which it can be withdrawn at a day or two's notice. Whether ease of withdrawal is important to an investor will depend upon his own particular circumstances and needs, but other things being equal it will be an added advantage to invest in something from which money can be withdrawn readily and with little fuss.

Not only is the speed with which capital can be realised important, but *the cost incurred in investing and withdrawing money* is also important. With some investments there is little or no cost incurred in depositing money and subsequently withdrawing it, but with others there may be considerable expenses to be met, such as the payment of professional fees and stamp duty, and sometimes even the repayment of a certain amount of interest as a penalty if the withdrawal of capital is premature. Obviously the cheaper it is to invest and withdraw money, the more attractive will be an investment.

It may be that an investor will wish to withdraw part of his money, but not the entire sum. If so it will be a great advantage if he is able to sell only part of the holding, but this is not always possible. For instance, if he has invested in a piece of property it may be impossible for him to sub-divide it and sell a portion of it, and the question of *whether an investment is divisible into smaller lots* which can be sold as and when convenient may be of considerable importance to an individual investor. This may be so even if the investor does not really expect to have to take such action, as the extra flexibility which the possibility of sub-division gives is an added attraction in an investment if all the other desired qualities are also present.

The first quality which was discussed was the security of the capital, and in times of inflation, when the purchasing power of money is rapidly decreasing, it is not only important that the capital which was originally invested should be capable of recoupment at any point in time, but also that the investment in which the money has been placed appreciates at a sufficiently rapid rate to keep pace with the changing value of money. An investor will wish to have his money in something in which capital appreciation enables him to withdraw it after a period of time and to purchase with that money the same amount of goods and services he could have purchased when the money was originally invested. If his investment is secure in this way it is referred to as being *secure in real terms*, as the real value of his money has been maintained. If his capital appreciates even more rapidly, the investment is of course still more attractive.

If the converse applies and he is unable to purchase as many goods at the end of the period of investment, then he will not really be as well off as he was originally, and his investment will not have been secure in real terms. When an investment is secure in real terms it is often referred to as being a good hedge against inflation, or as being inflation-proof. In recent years this quality has perhaps been the most desirable quality of an investment, and the fact that property has generally satis-fied this requirement has tended to make it a very attractive investment for those who require security in real terms. A cau-tionary word should be added at this stage to point out that not all types of property have fallen into this category, and undoubtedly there will be some types of property in the future which will not be secure in real terms. Nevertheless, it is gener-ally true to say that good property investments have possessed this quality to a greater degree than many other investments.

The overall risk attached to property will be a reflection of all the various qualities mentioned in the preceding paragraphs, and possibly also other qualities which the particular investor may consider important. Not all investors will place emphasis on all these features and, to some, certain qualities will be more important than others. One particular investment will not con-tain the same element of risk for all investors, and a person who wishes to have a high income yield may not be as worried about security of capital as another investor who must at all costs avoid losing any of his capital, but who has adequate income from other sources to satisfy his daily needs. The individual investor will decide his own preferences, and the risk will depend on a combination of those preferences related to the features of the particular investment.

Generally speaking the riskier an investment is considered to be, the higher the yield the investor will require before he can be tempted to place his money in it. In layman's terms, this means the riskier the investment the greater the return the investor will require. This is not unnatural, and is not dissimilar from the position a person might be in if he were asked to do a dangerous job. He would undoubtedly require higher pay than he would expect for a safer job, and the higher yield that an investor requires from a risky investment is to some extent danger money for placing his savings in an investment which may lose him capital.

Apart from the danger money aspect of investment, there will also be a desire to recoup the capital as rapidly as possible and in receiving a higher return an investor will be more rapidly decreasing his original outlay than if he receives a small annual return. Although this may only be a rough and ready way of judging the quality of an investment, it is nonetheless a practical consideration, and if a 25% return can be obtained from a risky investment, by the end of the fourth year the original capital will have been recovered and so, to this extent, the risk will have been somewhat decreased. Obviously, to consider the situation in this way is to ignore the fact that the annual payments are really his earnings for giving up the use of his money and are not capital repayments, and so strictly speaking this is not a mathematically correct way of assessing the quality of an investment, but it is nevertheless a useful rule of thumb method.

The reader may well be able to think of other qualities which may be of importance in different situations, but as this book is principally a consideration of property and property values, it is worth considering which of the above qualities are particularly evident in property investment, and also to consider their degrees of importance. There is little doubt, that over recent years the security of capital in real terms has been a particularly important feature. Indeed, in many instances capital has not only been secure in real terms, but marked capital appreciation has also been evident in many property investments. This has resulted in considerable capital gains being made on them, and this has naturally proved an attractive feature.

In good property investments the security and regularity of income has also been evident and where good quality property has been owned of a type for which demand has been high, there has been little likelihood of the income flow drying up or of rent not being paid on time. When such a misfortune has taken place, the property owner in most instances will have been able readily to re-let the property and his income flow will have resumed.

On the other side of the coin, it is not easy to sell property at short notice, and it may take many months, even years, to realize capital, as a property will not sell unless it fulfils the requirements of at least one potential purchaser. Because properties vary so much, it may be a considerable time before the purchaser who requires a particular property arrives on the scene, and this is a considerable disadvantage with property investment. It is also a fact that property is very often not divisible into smaller units, which is again awkward if only part of the original capital outlay needs to be recouped.

In recent years this indivisibility of property interests has proved a great problem with very valuable properties, so much so that the "unitisation" of property interests has occured (see Chapter 9).

Investment in property is therefore likely to be of interest to the investor who will not need to recoup his money over the short term, and who places a high priority on security of capital, particularly in real terms, and on a regular receipt of income.

The relative stability of the property market and the fact that most freehold interests in property (and even some leasehold interests) have shown considerable capital growth over the years in real terms as well as in absolute terms, make property interests attractive security for those lending money. This is an important feature of property and enables owners of interests to borrow money using those interests as security (collateral), using the borrowed money for business ventures. The ability to use property in this way is very important both to borrowers and lenders and is a very positive benefit of property ownership.

CHAPTER 4

INVESTMENT OPPORTUNITIES

There are many ways in which money can be utilised and the possibility of *expenditure on pleasure* has already been considered. Money which has been spent on pleasure is gone and cannot provide a future income-flow in the form of earnings, but if one's resources are sufficiently large for a regular income-flow to be of limited importance then this is not necessarily a great disadvantage. A person with large money resources may well decide that he can get the greatest enjoyment from life if he simply divides the money by the number of years he reasonably expects to live, and spends the resultant figure each year. He may have no dependants to worry about, and may well find this an exceedingly satisfying way of life. Although such a course of action may to some seem misguided, it must be remembered that there may be many who think otherwise, particularly if their philosophy of life is that to-day is more important than to-morrow.

Articles Bought For Use

These are of a more permanent nature and are likely to give returns over a longer period of time, but, even so, in most instances they will be wasting assets. They will wear out with time and will be less efficient as the years pass. They will also in all probability require regular expenditure on maintenance, and even on partial replacement.

Even so, many articles of this nature give great returns over substantial periods of time, and in that respect prove excellent investments. From household goods such as washing machines, to motor cars which give prolonged service both to individuals and businesses, to the plant and machinery essential for industrial production, all are articles bought for use which give great service over long periods, justifying both the initial capital expenditure and the essential periodic expenditure on them.

Stocks and Shares

If *stocks and shares* are purchased, a small part of a company is in fact purchased, the size and part owned being represented by the relationship between the shareholding bought and the total number of issued shares in the company (i.e. the number of shares in the company that have been sold in the market). So if 1,000 shares in a company are bought and there are 500,000 issued shares, 1/500 of the company is owned by the purchaser. This does not in itself give the shareholder the right to tell anyone in the company how to work, or to make any decisions which will bind the company. The day-to-day running of the company will be in most cases carried out by paid employees and a paid management staff, and the policy decisions will be made by a board of directors who will be elected by annual meetings of shareholders. However, as a part owner of the company, a share-holder will be entitled to a share in the company's profits, that is if it makes profits, and if the board of directors decides to distribute any of them. The board may decide to retain some of the profits within the company for such reasons as to provide for future taxation or for future expansion of the company's activities, but whatever profits it decides to distribute will be shared amongst the part owners according to the size of their shareholdings. The return to a share is known as the dividend, and this is one form of return that an investor will hope to get from stocks and shares, although the size of dividends and the regularity of payments will be uncertain and will depend upon the performance of the company concerned and the decisions of the board of directors.

If stocks or shares are bought in a progressive and prosperous company there is also likely to be capital appreciation. If a company commences with a given amount of capital and subsequently expands and builds up its capital resources, the value of the shares in the company will invariably increase. So not only will dividends be obtained from the company, but the capital will be secure and will increase in value. People want to be shareholders in successful companies, and as it becomes known that a particular company is very successful, so the desire of people to purchase shares in that company will push up their price in the stock market. Because of the increased demand, shares can be sold for considerably more than was originally paid for them. Obviously a share which pays good dividends and also offers the prospects of a capital gain will be more attract-ive than one which merely pays a good dividend, unless there happens to be such a rare bird as an investor who does not want a capital gain.

Capital appreciation does not always result from investment in stocks and shares. It is just as easy to get capital depreciation in the Stock Market—probably easier. This is not unlike backing horses in some respects; for every capital gain made there is probably someone making a capital loss, or at least not doing particularly well out of a transaction. That a winner has been backed does not alter the fact that others may be backing losers. There have been several very well known companies which have run into difficulties, which has highlighted the risks inherent in investment in the Stock Market—Rolls Royce and Lines Brothers, the well known toy-makers, are typical United Kingdom examples. There is a risk in investment in stocks and shares, but it is probably true to say that unless there are risks there will be little prospect of high returns. If one plays safe all the time one will not make a fortune, just as the batsman who always plays cautious strokes is not likely to hit boundaries—if he does occasionally do so there will in any case probably be no spectators to watch him and he will not be a financial success, just as the ultra-cautious investor is unlikely to die a millionaire. Backing the two to one odds-on winner at the races will not enable one to make a fortune, and because the risk is far greater there will be more money to be made from backing the 100 to 1 against runner, always assuming it wins. The greater the risk the greater the returns one can hope for, but also the greater the possibility of complete failure.

Perhaps the biggest advantage about investment in stocks and shares is that generally they are very easily marketable. A telephone call giving instructions to a bank manager or stockbroker is all that is needed, and providing the quoted price at which a sale or purchase can be made is satisfactory, the transaction can be rapidly completed. The London Stock Exchange has "account periods" of about two weeks in length, and payment for shares purchased, together with commission charged for carrying out the transaction and any stamp duty which has been incurred, has to be made at the end of the account during which the transaction took place. Likewise, the net sum due to an investor following a sale will also be paid at the end of the relevant account, and it can therefore be seen that one of the main virtues of investment in stocks and shares is that an investor can quickly and easily realise money, should the need arise.

Following the purchase of shares the share certificate may not be received until some months later, but once a contract has been completed for a transaction one is the owner of the relevant shares. They can be sold again before the share certificate is received, and, indeed, shares may well be re-sold within minutes of being purchased. This will normally only happen if a quick profit can be made, but it might also happen if an unfortunate blunder was made in purchasing, and the investor is attempting to cut his losses by immediately reselling. If purchases and sales are made within the same account the investor will simply receive a cheque from his broker at the end of the account for the difference between the net sums realised on sales and the total costs of his purchases, or alternatively he may have to pay the difference if his purchases cost more than sales realised.

However, one of the disadvantages of the Stock Exchange is that it is a volatile market, and, although it is easy to sell, a sale cannot necessarily be arranged at the right price. There is no guarantee that the original expenditure can be recouped. If a person is likely to want his money back quickly and cannot afford to lose any of it, then he should not invest on the Stock Exchange. Stock Exchange investments should only be made if the investor can afford to lose his money, as such a misfortune can easily occur. If it is known that a specific sum of money has to be available some time in the future it should not be invested in stocks and shares, because the capital could be worth considerably less at that future date than the sum originally invested. It is impossible to predict accurately what is going to happen on the Stock Market, so the investor must always be prepared for the unexpected, and must not complain if it happens. However, if money is available and its loss can be risked, and a careful study can be made of the market or a particular sector of it, then the Stock Market can provide rewarding and convenient investments.

National Savings Certificates

National Savings Certificates are issued by the British Government, other governments having similar savings devices. When certificates are bought the precise purchase price is known and also the rate of interest which will be paid whilst they are held, whilst the normal redemption value will be stated at the time of purchase. They are therefore convenient for the more cautious type of person, or for the person to whom circumstances dictate that caution is necessary, for there are times when even the most confirmed natural gambler should exercise a degree of caution. As they can be purchased in small units they are also attractive to people of limited means.

Such investments normally can also be redeemed at an early date at a sum which can be accurately calculated, so they have the advantages of being a relatively liquid form of holding capital with little uncertainty attached. Against this they do not generally give very high returns, and there is little capital appreciation to be obtained.

In order to overcome the disadvantage that investment in National Savings Certificates is likely to result in capital loss in real terms during a period of inflation, some certificates have been index-linked to the cost of living in recent years. Initially in the United Kingdom, index-linked certificates could only be bought by those who were 60 years old or older, but such rules can be and are varied with the passage of time and changes in circumstances.

Gilt-edged Securities

These are Government Stock, or Loan Stock which has been issued by a Government as a method of raising money to fund its own activities or in an attempt to regulate the economy. Governments offer stock in exchange for a loan from the purchaser, and in return promise to pay a certain annual rate of return, and in many cases to repay the original capital at a specific future date. In other cases the stock may be undated and there is no promise to repay the capital at any specific time, if at all. In such cases the investment becomes what is virtually a permanent loan, if the Government cares to treat it as such. The investor can nevertheless realise his capital by selling the stock on the Stock Exchange, but in this case he will not necessarily get the value of the original loan and will have to sell at the market rate for his particular stock at the time it is sold.

If the stock is dated, the Government promises to make repayment at some future date which may be quoted as a specific year, or a specific period of years, which would give the Government the option to choose the most favourable repayment date to them during that period. In the United Kingdom examples of the two types of repayment dates are 14% Treasury Stock 1996 and 12½% Treasury Stock 2003–05. With the first, interest of 14% per annum will be paid, and the nominal value of the stock will be repaid in 1996, whereas the second pays a rate of interest of 12½% and has a more distant repayment date sometime during a period of 3 years ending with 2005.

A major difference between gilt-edged securities and National Savings Certificates is that gilt-edged securities can be bought and sold on the Stock Market at prices which fluctuate, depending upon the prevailing market conditions. Consequently their value at any future date cannot be certain, and there is therefore a relative insecurity of capital attached to such an investment. With a dated stock there is security of capital in the long term, although not necessarily in real terms, and there may be insecurity in the short term before the redemption date is reached.

Debenture Stock

This is more usually referred to as "debentures" and is in fact loan stock issued by companies. A company may need to raise money and it may decide to do so by issuing debenture stock in return for loans from private investors who are willing to lend money to the company. Such a move provides an alternative source of fund-raising for the company as opposed to going to a bank or other institution, and, providing the company is healthy and flourishing, it will provide an investor in the debentures with a steady and reliable income-flow at a known rate of interest. This will be at a rate quoted by the company when the stock is issued, and will have been pitched at a level which the company hopes will attract investors' money. For a debenture issue to be favourably received by investors it must therefore be issued at or about the current market rate of interest at the time of issue. Any hope of capital appreciation for the investor must depend upon market rates of interest moving in a downward direction, in which case the yield on his debentures will be above the market rate and he will be able to sell his stock at a premium.

The holder of debenture stock is not a part owner of the company—he does not hold shares in the company, he merely lends money to it. If the company runs into difficulties he may possibly lose all the money he has lent, but on the other hand he will rank before the ordinary shareholders for the repayment of his loan; in such circumstances he will have a "prior charge".

Local Authority Loans

In the same way as companies may wish to raise money by borrowing, so also may local authorities. The terms of such loans are regularly advertised in the financial pages of the national press, when it is usual to see details of the rate of interest to be paid, the minimum size of loan accepted, and the minimum loan-period. As regards their quality as investments, they are very similar to debentures in their attributes, although it would be hoped that the possibility of a local authority being unable to repay loan stock would not exist.

Insurance Policies

An insurance policy is taken out to provide cover against the loss which could arise on the occurrence of an unlikely and unwanted event, which it is obviously hoped will not in fact occur. A premium is paid to the insurers, who agree to pay certain sums of money on the occurrence of the events insured against, the full details depending upon the full terms of the policy. In the simplest form of policy there is no return at all unless the event occurs, for example with a car policy there is no payment unless the car is damaged or stolen or someone is injured as a result of the use of the car.

An Assurance Policy is taken out to provide cover against an event which will assuredly occur, namely death. It is similar to an insurance policy in that there are no returns until the event occurs, when it will be someone other than the person suffering the damage who will receive the benefit of the insurance money.

An Endowment Policy is one in which, in return for paying a series of premiums over a period of time, or a single premium at the beginning of the period, the policy-holder is guaranteed the payment from the insurers of a certain sum at the end of that period. The sum payable may be a specific amount, or it may be expressed as a certain amount plus profits. In the latter case the quoted amount will normally be lower than if there is no share of the profits, for in addition to the lump sum quoted in the policy, the policy-holder will also be paid a proportion of the profits made by the insurance company during the term of the policy. In any event, the lump sum guaranteed by the insurance company will usually show a very low annual rate of interest when related to the premiums paid to the company, largely because payment is guaranteed. It may be that another reason is that many people who take out policies do so in ignorance of the low yield they are really accepting on their investment. Certainly, in the light of very high inflation in recent years, many endowment policies taken out some years ago have proved to be incredibly bad investments. Nevertheless, there is a large degree of certainty about them, as it is unlikely that most of the leading insurance companies will go bankrupt, although this has occured to some very well known companies in the relatively recent past.

A popular form of insurance policy is that which links life cover with an endowment. A quoted sum, which will comprise the money he pays to the company plus interest on that money, is guaranteed to be paid to the policy-holder when either the date quoted for the endowment has been reached or death occurs. This is perhaps the best type of policy to have, as with a little luck the insured person may enjoy the money himself. In return for a series of annual payments a young married man might be guaranteed the sum of £20,000 on death or in 35 years' time. In 35 years' time he will receive the money, but, if in the meantime he dies, his widow will receive the money on his death and premium payments will cease. If the death occurred when only one premium payment had been made the receipt of the lump sum would yield an incredibly high rate of return on the investment, a fact which would be of great help to the widow but of little help to the insured.

Although the indemnity cover of insurance is well worth having, it is debatable whether policies have much to recommend them as pure investments, judging by the way the purchasing power of the sum payable is eroded by inflation.

Linked Insurance

This is a type of investment which has come to the fore in recent years. Financial institutions realised the shortcomings of insurance policies which did not give adequate security in real terms, and various packages have been devised and offered on the market which give both insurance cover and participation in equity investment. Part of the premium provides for insurance, and the remainder is invested in equities, usually of a specified type or in a specified range of companies, the long-term hope being that the equity portion will give the investor growth which will at least keep his capital secure in real terms, and possibly even give him growth in real terms. This then is an investment which gives both the security which insurance offers and the prospect of capital growth which the ownership of equities offers, although it must be remembered that the dual-purpose nature of the investment must inevitably result in each of these qualities being less pronounced than if an investment were made solely in either insurance or equities. It does tend to be a long-term investment with a commitment to the payment of regular sums, and it may be that with the passage of time and changes in circumstances, such an investment may cease to be attractive or may become inconvenient. Also, the quality of the investment will depend upon the quality of the trust management, which will vary from trust to trust, and may even vary within one particular trust over a period.

Unit Trusts and Investment Trusts

These are somewhat similar, in that money is paid to buy shares in a Trust which in turn re-invests the money in stocks and shares. Both offer a convenient way in which small investors can spread the risk when investing in the Stock Exchange—they obtain a block of shares from the Trust which will hold the shares of many leading companies, probably selected from a variety of industries, and consequently they become what could be described as owners at second hand of a few shares (possibly even fractions of shares) in a great many companies. Without the facility of the Trust an individual would require a far larger amount of capital to be able to acquire holdings in such a large number of companies.

By re-investing the money in a variety of companies the Trust reduces the risk of an investor losing all his money, but at the same time it is probably true that the possibility of making very large gains is also decreased, as large capital gains on one share may well be countered by smaller gains and even losses on other shares. So investing in Trusts increases the security of capital and probably the security of income also, and enables the person with limited resources to obtain an interest in a wide range of companies.

There are several differences between Unit Trusts and Investment Trusts, but to the small investor the most important difference is probably the fact that capital can only be realised by selling holdings in Unit Trusts to the Trust managers at the price quoted by them at the time of sale, whilst holdings in Investment Trusts can be sold on the Stock Exchange at the current market rate, which can be readily ascertained through the financial press, a stockbroker or a bank.

Property Bonds

These are similar to linked insurance, which was discussed earlier, with the investment in equities being restricted to property shares. Property Bonds therefore enable an investor to get insurance cover and an interest in property shares at one and the same time, the importance of the property element being that many investors have in the past regarded property, and consequently property companies, as being one of the safest and most rapidly growing types of investment available.

However, though it is easy to assume that an investment in property cannot go wrong, it is important to remember that not all property investments are good. Again, the success of property bonds depends to a very large extent upon the quality of the management, and as the quality of bond managers and the quality of property investments approaches the margin between good and bad, then so will the quality of property bonds vary.

Property Shares

Some investors may decide to invest only in the shares of property companies, many of which have quotes on the Stock Exchange. Many of these companies have in recent years become almost household names, some because of the rapidity of their growth and the quality of their management and products, others because of adverse press publicity, some of which is justified, much of which is not justified, and a large proportion of which is simply ill-informed and misguided.

Because of the speed and size of growth many of these companies have become much favoured by investors, and the purchase of equities in property companies offers the small investor, who may not have sufficient resources actually to involve himself in property development and investment, the chance to share in someone else's involvement, and also, it is hoped, someone else's success. Whereas a considerable sum of money is needed before an interest in property can be purchased or a development scheme started, it is possible to purchase a holding of property shares for a relatively small figure.

Property
From investments of a general nature we have progressed to those with a property flavour, and as this is obviously a very important topic it will be covered in a later chapter at somewhat greater length than the other forms of investment.

At this stage it is sufficient to note that there are many types of property available for the would-be investor, and a variety of interests in such properties. There may be freeholds, short or long leaseholds, ground rents, offices, shops, factories, warehouses, farms and other types of property, and each of these interests or types of property will have features which make them more or less attractive to investors, depending upon circumstances and the requirements of the particular investor.

Several features of property investment which should be remembered when comparing it with alternative types of investment are:—

1. Property investment tends to be long-term in nature.
2. The costs of purchasing and selling property investments are relatively high.
3. The time involved in buying and selling is lengthy.
4. Proof of ownership can sometimes be difficult.
5. The amount of capital required to buy property is high, relatively speaking, and it is not often possible to buy part shares.
6. There may be considerable management problems involved in owning property.
7. Property seems to be prone to interference in the form of legislation by governments of all colours, and this can be extremely damaging to the value of an interest.
8. There can be considerable prestige to being a property owner.
9. Property values tend to appreciate with time, and property is therefore usually a good hedge against inflation.
10. The yield on property investments is generally much higher than the yield on a similar sum invested in other forms

of investment, this being compensation for some of the disadvantages listed above.

11. An interest in property can often be used as security (collateral) against which loan finance can be raised.

The particular features of property investments will be considered again in Chapter 9.

CHAPTER 5

PROPERTY INVESTMENT AND UNDERLYING FACTORS OF THE MARKET

As there are many factors which can affect property values and which should be considered by property investors, it is essential for valuers to study the property market at considerable length, and also the underlying factors which affect it.

The International Situation

Even the international situation can affect property values, and this was vividly illustrated by the events in the United Kingdom market during the years 1972 and 1973. In 1972 residential property values rose dramatically almost daily, to levels which would previously have been considered ridiculous, whilst there was a considerable reversal in 1973. Although prices did not fall to the levels of early 1972, there was nevertheless a considerable fall from the peaks of 1972, and many would-be sellers found difficulty in disposing of their properties. One of the major reasons for this was the shortage of mortgage funds in 1973 as opposed to the seemingly limitless supplies during 1972, and also the higher cost of borrowing as a result of world-wide increases in interest rates. So the international financial situation during this period had an important effect on the property market, as it did again in the period 1979–1981 when high international interest rates helped to make it expensive to borrow money. Not surprisingly, similar effects were evident in property markets in other countries as a result of the same high interest rates. There will also be occasions when the market will react to moods of optimism or depression on the part of investors which may well be caused by such things as the international political situation. The property market does not normally react in quite so volatile a manner as does the stock market, as property investment is essentially a long-term investment and investors are therefore influenced more by long-term prospects than by short-term ups and downs. However, there is much to suggest that even the latter can have repercussions in the property market, and, of course, the longer or stronger the mood of optimism or depression, the greater will be its effect.

The National Situation and Finance

National affairs are also very important in influencing the mood of investors, and the state of a national economy is very important. If a boom period appears to lie ahead, investors will be confident, while if future prospects appear gloomy, they will be far from confident, and such factors must make a terrific difference to the type of investment into which investors are prepared to put their money. Apart from affecting the thinking of investors, the economic situation can also affect the amount of money in circulation at any particular moment of time. The stringent credit restrictions in the United Kingdom in the late 1960's prevented many people from going ahead with schemes which appeared promising, purely and simply because they could not obtain the necessary finance. There was none to lend, and without money there could be no scheme. The quality of the investment as a risk was irrelevant, as even very reputable people could not obtain finance.

In 1971–1972 the situation was quite different and lower interest rates made borrowing cheaper. With plenty of loan money available in the economy, there were more would-be buyers with funds available, and this was a major factor in the surge of property prices in 1972.

The amount of money available and the cost of borrowing can also affect the preferences of an investor, as well as determining whether he can afford to purchase or not. Having decided that he can obtain finance to make a purchase, if borrowing costs are low and if he can borrow a large sum, he may well decide to invest in bigger and better investments than if the converse had been the case. Likewise, if everything in the garden appears rosy with plenty of money available, an investor may well be so optimistic as to go for riskier investments whose potential pay-off, if all goes well, is very high. If things generally appear tighter, the investor will be more likely to be attracted by the lower yielding and safer investment, and, if he is likely to need his money back at short notice, liquidity of capital will probably become the most important factor.

In the period 1978–1981 there was a serious world economic depression. The British economy, like many others, suffered with high interest rates, high rates of inflation, depressed industrial production and rising unemployment. These factors influenced investment in property both in terms of the amount of investment which actually occurred during that period and the investment preferences of those investing.

The expected trend in the economy is also important in influencing investors. If current yields are high but in the long term they are expected to become lower, an investor may be keen to tie his money up in a high-yielding long-term investment. However, if current yields are low but in the long term are expected to rise, then it is better for the investor to put his money into an investment from which he can readily withdraw it for re-investment when interest rates rise.

Government Policies

Government policies are extremely important to investors. In many instances Governments have given direct aid, such as grants to farmers for various purposes, and improvement grants, which have been given to encourage the improvement and modernisation of older residential properties. There is little doubt that such aid influences investment policy, as with the aid of a grant a scheme which previously was unremunerative and unattractive may suddenly become a paying proposition. Likewise the removal of a system of grants will probably have the converse effect, unless, having become involved with a particular line of investment, the investor has obtained sufficient knowledge and expertise to realise that even without a grant it is still worthwhile. Government policies of this type will inevitably influence the property market, even when they relate to other forms of investment, as there may well be a diversion to or from property investment as a result of factors affecting other investments.

In the United Kingdom Budget of 1980 the Chancellor of the Exchequer, Sir Geoffrey Howe, announced the introduction of Enterprise Zones. Briefly, these were to be a number of selected areas, relatively small in size, where it was thought preferential treatment would be desirable to encourage industrial and commercial regeneration. Amongst the benefits for those developing in these zones would be the removal of planning restrictions and requirements, and preferential tax treatment. It is clear that such measures make the Zones more attractive for investment and development than neighbouring and other areas which do not have such advantages. As a result their creation is likely to have a considerable effect on the decisions of those contemplating property investment and development in the localities of Enterprise Zones.

Another obvious way in which government policy affects investment, and property investment in particular, is in respect of statutory policy, and this will be discussed in a later chapter.

The Local Economy

The state and trends in the local economy will be of prime

importance. An investment in property in a depressed area is hardly likely to be as attractive as a similar investment in a thriving area, unless the depressed area currently offers investment possibilities at bargain-basement prices and it is considered that future prospects for the area are good, or unless, as in Enterprise Zones, inducements are offered to make investment worthwhile. Investment in a brand new sports stadium and entertainments centre generally would be inadvisable in an area of high unemployment, particularly if the limited employment which did exist in the area provided a low average income. Such an investment would be best reserved for areas of high employment and high incomes.

Geographical Factors

There are many geographical factors which influence the values of properties, and although many or all of them may appear obvious, it is nevertheless important to consider them, as it is often the obvious that is overlooked.

The *latitude* of the area may be important if the use of a property is likely to be affected in any way by the warmth of the climate or the length of seasons. A farm in the south-west of England will be suitable for a different type of farming from one in the north of Scotland, whilst a hotel in the former area will normally expect a longer summer season than one in the latter area. Likewise, the existence of a swimming pool in the grounds of a house is likely to cause a higher increment in value if the house is in a warm location rather than if it is in a colder area.

Topography—whether an area is flat or hilly, the existence or absence of rivers, and similar factors, may well have an important effect on value. The existence of geographical obstacles such as hills and rivers might well determine the catchment area of a shopping centre, whilst they could also create quite substantial price differences in the housing market. In an age of increasing affluence and leisure the existence of river frontage, particularly if it has good fishing rights, can make a house extremely valuable, whereas in earlier, less affluent times, and before the various local river authorities were so active in cleaning out rivers, it could well have been a positive disadvantage because of the danger of flooding.

The *aspect* of a property may be important, particularly in residential areas. Advertisements for houses often emphasise the fact that they are "facing south" or "built on the southern slopes of . . .", whilst if the objective were to try to grow vines in the United Kingdom a southern-facing slope would be a great help, if not essential. Another way in which aspect is important is in respect of the outlook of a house, any property which overlooks a pleasant area obviously being more attractive than one which overlooks unattractive surroundings.

Local climatic conditions may vary considerably, and the value of properties will probably vary with them. Cotton and woollen industries have in the past often developed in particular areas because of certain features of the local climate which favoured their establishment. In hill areas there are often considerable differences in annual rainfall within the space of a few miles which may greatly influence the pattern of residential settlement. At Minehead in Somerset the average annual rainfall is 35 inches, whilst a few miles inland at Dulverton it is 60 inches, and it is 80 inches on the nearby hills of Exmoor.

Other Factors

The existence of good *communications* and accessibility have always been important in influencing value, and it is no less so to-day. Even though modern vehicles can travel fast, it is still an advantage to be close to good means of communication.

Some time ago I inspected a house set in a remote moorland area. The advertisement and the sales particulars both sounded very interesting and the property itself proved to have many attractive features, being set in a really beautiful and peaceful location close to a pretty trout stream and having several acres of land. However, to reach it involved a drive of about one mile across an unmade moorland road and through a ford which was quite deep even in the middle of a dry spell. The probability was that it would be cut off for several weeks each winter, and any prospective purchaser would need to equip himself with a cross-country vehicle and a large deep-freeze in which to store provisions, apart from having the type of temperament which would allow him to stand real solitude.

The property did not sell that summer, and it is possibly still empty. The one major disadvantage was its inaccessibility and distance from good means of communication, and this effectively "killed the market".

The closure of local railway lines and stations may well result in a change of values, particularly in an age when so many local 'bus services also seem to have closed down, or, where they still exist, are expensive to use.

Good communications are vital with commercial properties, particularly industrial and warehouse units, and it is common to see the proximity to a motorway access point stressed as the most important feature. A warehouseman storing perishable goods will not want them to go rotten in transit to the retailer, whilst in a competitive society any advantage of accessibility may enable a businessman either to undercut his rivals or to make a higher profit by virtue of the lower costs he incurs. Indeed, he may do both.

An office user often needs to be close to or accessible to others with whom he does business, and it is also necessary for offices to be so located that staff can travel with ease to and from the premises, so making it easier to attract staff to work there. If staff can travel to work easily, and there is not the harrowing journey to work that is often a feature of modern life, it may even be possible for an employer to pay comparatively low wages and still have a happy work force, particularly if the office block is pleasantly located as well as accessible.

There is the possibility that the development of micro-processors may result in more office work being done by employees from their own homes, with a central office being used mainly for co-ordinating the work of the various "out-workers". It will be interesting to note whether such a trend develops, as if it does it could well result in the accessibility of an office block being a less important factor in determining value than previously. In effect, offices which are at present relatively inaccessible by road or rail could become relatively more accessible for communication by micro-processor.

Whereas in the past rivers, roads, canals and railways have at one time or another been the most important means of communications, it is probably true that the road network, and particularly the motorway network, is now the most important. The existence of good port facilities are important for international trade, as also are airport facilities to a growing degree, and possibly at some future date the Channel Tunnel may also be important.

Fashion and local demand are important, even though they are rather vague and difficult to assess. The stage is rapidly being reached in certain areas of the housing market in which buyers simply are not interested in a house which does not have a second bathroom. A few years ago the possibility of such a situation arising would have been considered ridiculous, but with increasing affluence it has become fashionable, and convenient, to have a second bathroom. The house that lags behind the change in fashion will inevitably command a lower price than those which have kept pace with it.

Similarly, in affluent areas a second garage and central heating have almost become essential, although it is noticeable that this tends to be the case more in the south-east of England than in many other areas of the United Kingdom.

It may well be that a property is difficult to market because it has a design or appearance that has become unfashionable. Some of the semi-detached houses erected in Britain between the two World Wars or the over-ornate properties erected in the latter part of the last century often fall into this category. Many properties erected more recently have elevations which are bedecked with a wide variety of finishes—shiplapping, varnished timber, tile-hanging, and many others—and while such finishes are in fashion they will prove good selling features. However, if the fashion changes, and it may well do so, particularly when high maintenance costs begin to rear their ugly heads, such finishes may eventually prove to be a great disadvantage.

Fashion can dictate the popularity of residential areas. In recent years it has become fashionable to live in parts of London, such as Chelsea, which were previously regarded as less desirable, and in many areas there are now wealthy people living in modernised cottages which were once the homes of labourers, and which may even have been legally unfit for human habitation before they were modernised. Indeed, many wealthy people now live in mews cottages which were once the homes of horses.

In many provincial cities large areas of housing have been demolished because the fashion of buying up old and poor quality housing and improving and modernising it never caught on. But, in many areas of London similar houses now provide excellent and desirable residences because some far-sighted people saw the potential of such properties in areas where there were acute housing shortages. Indeed, in recent years official planning policy has recognised the potential for improvement in many older properties to the extent that policies of wholesale clearance and rebuilding have been forsaken for policies of improvement involving the renovation of existing properties to improve both the quality of the individual properties and the locality concerned.

The *individual features of a property* are of importance in determining its value. Does it have a good or a bad design, is it functional, is it adaptable? A factory into which it is difficult to install modern equipment because of the difficulty of access, the small size of the doors, the low load-bearing capacity of the floors or the restricted clear working height, is obviously relatively unattractive in these days. A factory which is nice to work in is more likely to maintain a high value, just as is the case with a house.

In some instances a period design adds a huge sum to the value of a house, particularly if it is in an area which is noted for such houses and which is fashionable. However, the same features in a high street shop in a market town could be a positive disadvantage. When modern marketing techniques dictate that alterations should be made, if the property is a listed building it may be impossible to bring it up to modern retailing standards.

Several years ago there was great demand for new houses of modern design, and such properties sold readily whilst older properties stood on the market for many months and eventually fetched much lower prices. Later, purchasers realised that the majority of older properties were built to more spacious dimensions, and it became the fashion to purchase such houses and modernise them, whilst trying to retain their inherent character. The fact that the features of spaciousness and character became popular resulted in houses which possessed such features regularly commanding high prices on the market, thus illustrating the importance of fashion and trends in demand. Following the advent of the energy crisis and the resultant increased cost of heating, houses which were unduly spacious became relatively unattractive to purchasers, not only because of the increased cost of heating but also because of the high cost of rates on space which cannot necessarily be fully utilised. In countries in which property rates are levied on site value rather than on the value of buildings the latter factor would not be a consideration which affected the cost of occupation.

The *state of repair* will influence a purchaser, for if a property is in bad condition he cannot contemplate a purchase unless the price will enable him to cover the cost of reinstatement and, preferably also make a profit. If this is not the case he would be well advised to purchase a similar property which is already in better condition. The property which is in good condition will invariably sell more readily and at a higher price than that which is in bad condition.

The term *"services"* covers such items as mains gas supply, mains electricity, mains water, mains sewers, and to a lesser extent the existence of a telephone connection, and the presence or absence of these items must influence a potential purchaser. The idyllic country cottage will probably seem a little less attractive when it is discovered that at present there is only a chemical closet at the bottom of the garden, water is from a spring which has been known to run dry, lighting is by oil lamp, and mains electricity will cost a considerable sum to connect, whilst a telephone connection will also be expensive.

Although it is possible to live without all these modern conveniences, it is doubtful whether it is possible to carry on industrial activities without them, and it could well be that land which was physically suitable for industrial development is completely blighted by the lack of services. If services are available near to a property but connection to them is likely to be expensive, then it is almost inevitable that the market value of the property will be lower than if those services were already installed.

The *potential* of a property can greatly affect its attractiveness on the market. It may be in poor condition, but if it is capable of improvement it may still sell readily at a good price. This is what happened to many cottages in certain areas of London and also to inferior cottages in rural areas which have now become the sought-after residences of the affluent. If, however, there is no possibility of improvement or the cost would be excessive, then the property will be unattractive to purchasers.

This factor of potential may be relevant in the industrial as well as the residential market. An industrialist may require a factory of 5,000 m² in a particular location. He may well be unable to obtain a unit which satisfies both these requirements, and in such a case a 4,000 m² factory in the right location with adequate room for expansion to the required size may be more attractive than the right sized factory in the wrong location.

The capability and space for extension of a property may also be a great selling factor in the residential property market.

It often happens that old factories too large for the requirements of modern producers are disposed of, and if it is possible for them to be split up into a number of smaller units of the size demanded by would-be tenants or purchasers, the total value of the property may thereby be greatly increased.

Whenever one has to value a property or advise a client one should consider whether the property is currently being used to its greatest potential and, if not, the possibility of putting it to a higher use should be given careful consideration.

The *time element* may be critical, particularly in periods of rapid inflation such as the late "60's" and early "70's". A price which seems high at the commencement of a development scheme may be just about right by the time the scheme is completed, and a year or two later it may seem ridiculously low. An example of this is the case of contemporary style bungalows which were built in a coastal resort, the price on completion being advertised as £13,500. This seemed very high even though they were built to a high specification, as other bungalows offering a similar amount of accommodation were on the market for about £8,500. The properties were eventually sold for figures in the region of £12,500 about 18 months after first being advertised. Within another two years similar properties were changing hands at between £20,000 and £25,000, whilst the passage of another ten years has seen these prices trebled. Time made all the difference, many of the underlying market factors having changed in the interim period.

Time is also important to the valuer, as it is often easy to fall into the trap of not moving with the times. Valuers with many years' experience have been known to make comments such as "It went for £60,000, but it's never worth it". But the property must have been worth this sum to someone, otherwise that figure would not have been obtained. The valuer possibly made the mistake of not realising that value may change with time, and he may have had in mind the sum that the property obtained on an earlier sale some years previously. Alternatively, he may have made the mistake of associating his idea of value with the costs which he knew were incurred in originally creating the property, or of placing his own subjective valuation on the property rather than an objective assessment of what would be paid in the open market.

It should not be forgotten that properties may lose value with time, although in inflationary times this is the exception rather than the rule. Nevertheless, the further passage of time could result in the property of the last paragraph only fetching £50,000 on a subsequent sale. The doubting valuer might then consider his doubts well justified and the original purchase to have been at an ill-advised figure. This will not alter the fact that at the earlier date £60,000 was the market value.

Because of the time-factor it is always most important for the valuer to state clearly the date on which he makes a valuation. Property prices could vary incredibly in the space of a week because of exceptional circumstances. In Reading, England, a development of new houses sold with little difficulty, but within a week of the sale of some of them a scheme for a Motorway (Freeway) Link Road was announced. This was to go straight through some of them and extremely close to others. Most of these houses became virtually unsaleable overnight, and the value of those that were to remain decreased immediately. Time is important and may witness great and rapid changes.

It is always as well to remember that because of the *lack of market information* which exists in many property markets, properties often fetch prices which, with better information, a purchaser would not have paid. However, most property transactions are of a confidential nature, which explains the reluctance of valuers to reveal details, although much could be done to make more information available without violating confidentiality. It sometimes happens that for various reasons a person must have a particular property, and to forestall other possible purchasers he pays a price which in reality is above the figure for which he could have obtained it. Should he subsequently have to sell the property because of a change of circumstances, there is no guarantee that the same figure will be obtained if buyers then in the market do not have the same pressing reasons for purchase. Such a possibility should be considered fully, particularly in valuing for mortgage purposes.

It is not suggested that the underlying conditions and factors considered in this chapter are completely comprehensive, and the reader will doubtless be able to think of other points. Nevertheless, those mentioned should be sufficient to illustrate the complexity of the background to property values, without, it is hoped, putting the would-be valuer off for ever.

The relevant factors will be different in different cases, but in all instances it will be important for the valuer to consider carefully all the features of a property, both its advantages and disadvantages, before he can reach any decision on its overall merit and value.

CHAPTER 6

VALUE

The word "value" has already been used many times in this book, but what does it really mean? When a valuer uses the word he will normally be referring to "market value", which can be defined as the "money obtainable from a person or persons willing and able to purchase an article when it is offered for sale by a willing seller". There is no compulsion on either the vendor or the purchaser to enter into a transaction. The vendor will only sell if he obtains the sum he requires and the purchaser will only buy if he can do so at what he considers a satisfactory price. They are both willing parties to the transaction because they both consider the deal to be to their own personal advantage. The expression "market value" can be defined in many different ways, but the important thing is to grasp the concept rather than to remember any particular form of words.

Scarcity gives rise to value, and, generally speaking, when scarcity increases so will value increase. If articles in general demand become scarce, their value will normally increase; if there is no scarcity of an article there is likely to be little or no value attached to it. It is unlikely that one would be able to sell a bucket of water in India in the middle of the monsoon, but a person who had been lost without water in the middle of a desert might well be prepared to give all his worldly goods for a similar bucket of water. Similarly, air is free on the surface of the earth, where it is usually plentiful, but in a mine, where there is a lack of fresh air, it is invaluable, and much money may be spent to ensure that a regular supply of fresh air is available within the mine.

The same basic principle applies in the property market, and, all other things being equal, as the supply of a particular type of property increases so will the market value decrease, and vice versa. In the real world all other things rarely remain equal, and it is invariably found that both supply and demand are changing at the same time. The concept of value is nevertheless important, as the value of an article at any point in time shows the price at which supply and demand are equal—the price at which buyers and sellers who are prepared to do business are equal in number.

The value of an article therefore gives an indication of both the degree of scarcity of that article and of its utility when compared with other articles. Thus, in theory, one would expect people to pay more for articles which are very useful than for those which are less useful, although in practice this may not always be the case, if only because theory and practice often seem to be poles apart. Practice may often be based on imperfect knowledge, which results in such apparent anomalies arising as people paying higher prices for less useful articles, whilst theory may only consider the ideal circumstances which rarely occur in real life.

If a whole range of prices paid in the market is studied a pattern of consumer choice can be seen, and in the housing market the fact that purchasers pay high prices for houses in certain areas shows that consumers prefer to live in those areas, and are prepared to pay for the privilege. In examining the prices that have been paid for properties the individual valuations of all the purchasers are considered. Before purchasing an article each potential purchaser will normally put his own valuation on it. If the asking price is the same or less than his valuation, he will consider it worth his while to buy it. If the asking price is above his subjective valuation then he will not feel he would get value for money and will not purchase the article. A subjective value is the value to the subject or person concerned.

It may be that the person whose initial subjective valuation is below the asking price subsequently revises it in an upward direction, and does in fact purchase the article concerned. This is not unusual, neither is it necessarily unwise. As an article may have different values to different people, so may its value to one individual vary according to circumstances and needs. Just as a pint of beer may have no value to a teetotaller but some value to a regular drinker, so may a pint be incredibly valuable to the person who has just played nine vigorous sets of tennis, but of no value, or even of negative value, to the same person if he has already consumed ten pints. Circumstances may well change, and the wise person will take changes into account in the decision-making process.

The property market, as any other market, is composed of a whole range of subjective valuations, each of which may be regularly changing. Those of both buyers and sellers combine and interact to give the general level of values. The price of an article in the market will depend upon this interaction and will tend towards the point at which the number of potential purchasers and that of potential sellers are equal.

CHAPTER 7

REASONS FOR VALUATIONS

In the earlier definition of "valuation" it was stated that it was the art or science of estimating the value for a specific purpose.... The expression "specific purpose" could refer to the fact that properties may be used for a whole range of different uses such as residential, commercial, or industrial. However, the real significance is that there can be a wide variety of reasons for requiring a valuation, and it is possible to have a whole range of different values for one property at one particular moment in time, dependent upon the purpose of the valuation.

A valuer may be asked what a property will fetch if sold, and he then uses his skill and experience to advise his client as to the likely selling price. This is a *valuation for sale*. In making it the valuer will consider all the likely purchasers in the market at that time and all the alternative properties available to them, and having done that he will estimate what price would result from the competition between the various potential purchasers.

A client may request a valuation because he is considering the purchase of a property. *A valuation for purchase* should not be quite as far-ranging in scope as one for sale, for although the range of people interested in the property may be just as great, the valuer's considerations must be directed towards the requirements and finances of one person—his client. In such circumstances the needs and personal characteristics of his client may result in a different decision from that which might result from considering the entire market. The client's subjective requirements may result in the value being lower to him than to others in the market whose subjective requirements are different. Conversely, they may result in his outbidding the market for a property which fits his requirements exactly, but which would be a compromise for other potential purchasers.

It may be that a valuation is required for *mortgage* purposes. At this stage the reader may not know what a mortgage is, but, briefly, it is a loan for which the security is an interest in property. Most people who purchase property have insufficient cash to pay all the purchase price. They pay as much as they can afford out of their own funds, borrowing the balance from some person or institution which has money to lend. The lender will not wish to lend money unless he has some sort of security and can be relatively certain that he will get his money back should anything go wrong with the transaction. The loan is "secured" upon the property which is being purchased and the lender will be able to stake a claim for his money out of the value of the "mortgaged" property should the borrower default in any way.

The major objective in a mortgage valuation is to decide what sum a property is likely to fetch if a forced sale is necessary. When this is the case it is not always possible to put a property on the market at the most favourable time, or in the most favourable circumstances. The valuer therefore has to take a cautious view and has to decide what figure might be obtained in adverse conditions. Such a figure may differ considerably from that applicable to a valuation for sale, which in the majority of cases would only envisage a transaction being made in favourable circumstances. A valuation for mortgage purposes is a valuation for a lender who will not wish to take undue risks.

A valuer may be required to value a property for *rental* purposes because a client wishes to rent it. He must take into account what his client can afford to pay for the use of the property, and a figure of annual value will be required as opposed to a capital figure. The client must be advised what rent is appropriate and consideration must be given to what has been obtained for similar accommodation. It may be that a client is only able to obtain the property by paying what is considered to be more than he can afford or, alternatively, more than the property is worth to him. In such cases he will undoubtedly be advised only to do so if he can obtain a lease at the high rent for a relatively long period of time, as with time inflationary tendencies in the property market may in fact result in the original rent becoming low.

So the valuer will be influenced by the terms of a prospective lease as well as by physical factors such as the quality of the area and the property itself. A tenant will expect to pay a lower rent if he is responsible for repairing the property than if the landlord is going to do these repairs for him. If there are onerous restrictions governing the use of the property a potential tenant will similarly decrease his bid, and it is therefore important for the valuer to be fully aware of the purpose of the valuation and all the factors which are liable to be important.

A valuation for *Insurance* demands a completely different approach. The market value of the property becomes to a large extent irrelevant, and the valuer has to calculate what it would cost to replace the bricks and mortar should the building or part of it be destroyed. He measures the building, calculates its size, and then applies appropriate costings to the various building works which would be entailed in replacing it, and in this way he finds the cost of replacement, or the "value" of the building for insurance purposes. The actual value of the building if offered for sale on the market may be well in excess of this figure, if for no other reason than the fact that the market value includes the site as well as the building. It may alternatively happen that open market value is below the insurance "value", and this may occur where a building is rather ornate for its purpose, or is built of extravagantly expensive materials or to an expensive design.

Valuations are sometimes required for *balance sheet* purposes, when a company publishes its annual accounts, or for *redevelopment* purposes when someone thinks there may be redevelopment potential and wishes to have their views either confirmed or rebutted. Property may require valuing as an *asset* of a business if it is used for business purposes and the value of the business, including the property, has to be established. When a public authority wishes to acquire a property it is necessary to value it for compensation for *compulsory purchase*. A valuation for *rating* purposes may be needed where local taxation is concerned. When someone dies it may be necessary to value a property for *probate* purposes, that is to find the value upon which tax payable at death is to be assessed (inheritance tax in the United Kingdom). In each of these cases there will be different considerations to take into account, many of the valuation criteria being dictated by law in some cases. As many of these valuations entail a considerable knowledge of advanced valuation methods and a not inconsiderable legal knowledge, they will not be discussed further in this book.

Although it is apparent that there may be a whole range of different values in any one property at any one time, depending upon the reason for the valuation, it should be remembered that there will only be one *market price*.

CHAPTER 8

LEGAL INTERESTS IN PROPERTY

It can be seen that the study of valuation is not quite as straight-forward as might at first be imagined. Each different type of valuation may involve different techniques and different techni-cal knowledge, and it is necessary to make a searching study of many subjects which affect property and property values.

One of these subjects is law. It was stated earlier that "valua-tion is concerned with a particular interest in property at a parti-cular moment of time". Property itself cannot be owned—at law an interest in property is owned, which is somewhat different from owning the property itself. If the latter were possible there could normally only be one owner of a particular property at any one time (unless there happened to be joint owners). With interests in property it is possible for there to be many different interests in the same piece of property, each interest owned by a different person, and so there may be a hierarchy of interests at any one time, e.g. freehold, leasehold, sub-leasehold. The freeholder is the person who is usually regarded by the layman as the owner of a property, but in law each of the persons with a legal interest in the property is an owner.

A freeholder may not wish to use a property himself but may have purchased it as an investment, and he may decide to split it into several parts physically and to let the various parts to different lessees. Each of them will own a legal interest in the property if all the correct legal formalities have been attended to. In time one of the lessees may decide that he no longer wishes to use the property and, providing the terms of his lease permit such an action, he may sublet part or all of the property which he leases. In such a case there will be three legal interests in that part of the property. As far as the entire property is con-cerned, the legal interests created will have resulted in it being divided on what might be referred to as both a horizontal basis and a vertical basis, i.e. separate interests have been created both at one level and at inferior levels. If the freeholder had purchased the property with the aid of a mortgage the mortgagee would also have a legal interest in it. It is not unusual to find on investigation that the legal interests in even relatively small properties are numerous.

When a lessee disposes of his entire legal interest to a third party, the transaction is known as an assignment of the interest, and the purchaser is known as the "assignee" of the lease.

From the valuer's point of view, if there are several interests in one property at one time, each interest will almost certainly have a different value, barring coincidence or absolutely identical circumstances, and the former will probably occur more often than the latter.

He will therefore have to ensure, before making a valuation, that he is quite certain what interest he is to value, and what are the terms on which the relevant interest is owned. Whenever possible, he should personally examine the deed or lease, as he may notice details which are vital as far as value is concerned, but which might not be thought important by a solicitor who is trained to notice legal detail and not to consider matters of value.

The valuer should also take care to specify quite clearly in his report what interest he is valuing, and to include in the report a summary of all the important legal points so that there can be no misunderstanding as to the basis on which a valuation has been made.

The law of property is a subject in itself and it is not the purpose of this book to cover it. The student would be well advised to read the subject in a good text-book, as a thorough grasp of this branch of law will prove invaluable to him in his career as a valuer.

CHAPTER 9

FEATURES OF PROPERTY AND THE PROPERTY MARKET

Probably the main feature of *property interests* is that, to use an economist's expression, they *are heterogeneous*, or, in plain man's English, they are all different. Apart from joint interests in the same property, there will probably never be two interests which are exactly the same, and even though there may be row upon row of semi-detached houses which are apparently similar, they will all be on different sites. Although this may seem a minute distinction between them, it nevertheless means that each of the properties will be different.

Often such a small difference may be irrelevant in market terms, but in some instances it will make a considerable difference to the market value. The fact that certain houses are close to a school or a bus stop may be a distinct advantage, whereas others may be remote from these conveniences, although similar in all other respects. Other houses which are immediately adjacent to the school or bus stop may in turn suffer from the nuisance caused by such neighbours. So, along a street of basically indentical houses, there may be differences in value resulting simply from their closeness to or distance from other property users.

Even when a new estate of basically identical houses is constructed, within a very short period of time differences between the properties will invariably develop. One person may move in and add another garage to his house, another may build an extension on to his kitchen, another may add a shower room, whilst yet another owner may instal double glazing or roof insulation. The variations are almost limitless, and the stage is very soon reached in which nearly all the properties have many detailed differences.

Similarly, with shops there are rarely two identical properties. Many built-up areas have shopping streets constructed around the turn of the century in which, from the street itself, the properties all appear to be similar. From the rear or from internal inspection many differences may be revealed, and it often turns out that nearly all the shops have been substantially altered during the passage of time. A shopkeeper who requires much storage space and much showroom space may build an extension over the rear yard of the property. Another shopkeeper may knock

out partition walls in the main building to make it more suitable
for his purposes. Other shopkeepers may also have built extensions at the rear, some smaller than that built by the first shopkeeper, others larger. An inspection of the various alterations
and extensions may show that even where similar areas have
been added, the type and quality of construction may vary. A
number of shops which from the front appear similar may, therefore, on inspection all prove to be different to a significant degree.

Another important feature of *property is* that, relatively speaking it is *durable*. Many goods wear out and deteriorate rapidly,
but property normally lasts for many years with a very slow
rate of deterioration. Even when a property is so old that the
deterioration is considerable, it is often found that the value of
the land on which it stands has appreciated at a greater rate
than the rate of depreciation in the value of the building. The
result is that although the quality and physical condition of the
building has deteriorated, the overall value of the land and buildings has been maintained, and more often than not has
increased. In this respect property is quite different from most
other investments; *it* is very durable over time and *affords very
good security for money over a long period.*

In comparison with other goods a *large amount of capital is
usually required to purchase property.* Even the meanest interest
will usually require a considerable amount of money for its purchase, and allied to this is the fact that *property is often in units
which cannot easily be divided into smaller units.* The result is that
the minimum sum required for property purchase is usually quite
substantial, and it is necesary for a potential investor in land
and buildings to be able to raise such a sum before he can in
fact realise his ambitions. If a piece of cheese is purchased, should
the original piece which the grocer weighs be too heavy for the
customer, he merely cuts some off to leave a lower priced piece.
More often than not, such a solution is impossible with a property
if it proves to be beyond the means of the would-be purchaser.

Sometimes it is possible to split buildings up into smaller units
by using a little imagination and possibly by making minor structural adaptations. This may enable persons with smaller funds
to purchase them, but often such a course of action is not possible
and a would-be purchaser has to raise sufficient funds to buy
the entire property or he cannot purchase at all.

The market value of some properties has become so great that
it is difficult for even very large organisations to purchase them.
Not only is it difficult to raise the large sums of money required,
(in 1987 the long leasehold interest in the Regent Hotel in Sydney
sold for $140 million at which figure there could only have been

a limited number of potential purchasers but which already seems cheap in comparison with subsequent sales) but purchase of a property worth many millions of dollars or pounds may result in too great a proportion of an investment portfolio being held in one property. This may be an unattractive proposition and the very high value of some properties may in any event make them almost impossible to sell rapidly if good management policy so demands. The solution of purchase of very expensive properties by syndicates is not necessarily a good solution, as the portfolio management needs of syndicate members may vary considerably at any time, and whereas one syndicate member may, for example, wish to sell a property, other members of the syndicate might wish to retain it. Also, they might not wish to have certain possible purchasers of shares as syndicate members.

There has, therefore, recently been consideration in a number of countries where such practices do not currently exist of the possible unitisation of property interests. With unitisation it is possible for a legal interest in a property to be divided into a number of units of ownership, just as the value of a company is represented by a number of shares in it. Units in a property can then be bought and sold thus allowing each owner of units to pursue independent portfolio management policies. It also enables the value of very expensive properties to be broken down into units which are within the purchasing range of a great many more organisations, with the result that sales of interests in such properties are not dependent upon the ability of a small number of potential purchasers to raise incredibly large sums of money. Such a development will provide a more active market in interests in the more valuable properties and will prevent ownership being an unwieldy burden which few are able or willing to accept.

Proof of ownership of property can cause problems, and it is often a quite difficult, lengthy and costly process to prove ownership of a particular interest satisfactorily. The owner of a pen who wishes to sell it proves his ownership principally by possession and the fact that he carries the pen around with him. If he can also produce a receipt showing when and where he purchased it, this will usually be more than adequate to satisfy any would-be purchaser. Even with larger articles such as a motor-car proof of ownership is still relatively simple. With a car the mere fact of possession is generally a good indication and if it can be backed up by possession of the registration book and a receipt for the purchase money this will invariably be sufficient.

Where property is concerned, possession is not always indicative of ownership, and it is obviously impossible to pick up a piece of

property and carry it around. Many properties have several interests existing in them, each of which is capable of a transfer of
ownership, and to establish ownership of any particular interest
the possession of Title Deeds is necessary. These will not always
be simple and straightforward to understand, and there are
sometimes omissions in them. It may be that on a transfer of
ownership there will be lengthy work involved in the investigation of the precise details of ownership, some of which may
never be cleared up to the complete satisfaction of all concerned.

As a result *the costs of transfer are invariably relatively high* when
interests in property change hands. A skilled solicitor should
be employed to undertake such work (it can be done by individuals themselves but this is generally inadvisable), and quite
understandably a skilled professional will require adequate
remuneration for his services.

Because of the need to look into the legal history of a property
and the complexities which may arise, *much time is usually involved
in transferring interests.* A transaction with most types of goods
can be carried to completion within, at the very most, a matter
of days. Although in theory it is possible for transfers of property
also to be completed within a few days, in practice this rarely
occurs, as ideal circumstances seldom exist, and the time
involved in property transfer tends to run into weeks, or even
months.

*Another feature of the property market is that normally it does not
consist of one large market,* but of a series of smaller markets, each
of which is local in nature. Even within local markets the knowledge of property transactions tends to be far from perfect, and
purchasers and vendors suffer from a shortage of information
concerning past transactions. *The property market* is what economists call *an imperfect market,* and the imperfection of knowledge
becomes even more critical if an area in which a valuer has to
work is not familiar to him. A person may have made many
transactions in one locality over a long period of time, but if
activities are moved to another area some way away he is in
the position of having to start from scratch in garnering background information about that new market. In such circumstances it will probably be much quicker and simpler for the
investor to go direct to an expert in that local market, and to
employ an experienced and competent surveyor to advise him.
This again will result in *expense on professional fees,* which would
not be necessary if dealing with goods which have a relatively
uniform value throughout the whole of the country. In the latter
case the expert in one local market will also be sufficiently well
versed to operate in another local market, but where property

is concerned an investor will normally have to allow for the costs of professional advice in calculating his overall expenses, unless he himself happens to be sufficiently expert to do his own work.

Property can provide a source of income, and in this respect it is different from many other durable possessions. Because of this the ownership of property is often attractive to investors as well as to would-be users of the property. It provides an opportunity for a person to save money, and having saved it to purchase something which then provides a regular income. This income is a direct result of, and the reward for, the original saving or the deferment of immediate consumption. Consequently property is often a particularly attractive investment for savers.

Another feature of the property market is that *the total supply of land is to all intents and purposes fixed*, although land reclamation may provide marginal increases in the total supply. Supply is not necessarily fixed in a particular use, but the total supply of land is fixed, and strict planning control has in effect tended to restrict the supply of additional land to a particular use. Although land may not be physically restricted to a use, planners have in fact laid down rather rigid rules about what may be done and where it may be done. Because of this, and also because building is not normally a rapid process, an increase in the supply of a particular type of property can normally only take place over a relatively long period. Things happen more slowly in the property market than in most other markets. Consequently it will only attract people who can afford to let things happen slowly.

In the short run it may be possible to increase the supply of a particular type of property by conversion from one use to another. If there is a need for offices and there are not enough available, a spacious Georgian house could be converted into offices. But, again, it is normally only possible to take such action if planning permission for a change of use is obtained, and it may be that although market demand suggests that more offices are required, the local planning authority may not agree to their being provided.

It can therefore be seen that *the supply side of the property market cannot react very rapidly to changes in demand.*

Basic demand factors must also be considered. As *property fulfils a basic need of mankind* there will always be a reasonably strong demand for it. Everything that man does requires either land upon which to do it, or buildings and land. People live in houses; they work in buildings; those who work outside work on land, and even those who fly for a livelihood need land to take off from and to land on. So land fulfils a basic need of man, and those who own and manage this essential commodity are important people, more so in an advanced society. This is becoming more and more apparent with the passage of time, although it is only in the relatively recent past that land-use has been considered on a long-term basis other than by the more enlightened estate owners. Land is a valuable asset, and it is likely that great attention will be paid to land management policies in the future.

CHAPTER 10

FACTORS WHICH CAUSE CHANGES IN THE VALUE OF PROPERTY

As value is a function of supply and demand, a consideration of the factors which are likely to affect either the supply of or the demand for property is merited.

Any *increases or decreases in population* will obviously affect property values. If there is an increase, all other things being equal, demand will increase. A larger population will require more housing in which to live, more buildings in which to work, and more buildings for leisure-time activities and all the other ancillary activities associated with modern life.

Population changes may be considered on a national basis or on a more local basis, and if there are movements of population from one area to another property values are likely to be affected in both areas. Demand will increase in one area and it will decrease in the other, unless any other factors counterbalance such changes.

Changes in the age distribution of the population may affect property values. For example, in one period a large proportion of the population may be aged under 40, and in another period the majority of the population may be over 40. Such a change in age distribution will affect the type of demand, as, whereas older people probably demand more bungalows, younger people may be quite happy living in flats. It may be that the adaptation of the existing housing stock is sufficient to cater for such changes in demand, but it may equally well be that wholesale building is required.

Any change in the proportion of married people to single people will also be reflected in the demand for different types of properties, and hence in property values. Single people are more likely to be satisfied with one-room bed-sitters than are married couples, who, even if they are extremely happily married, will sometimes wish to have the privacy of a room to themselves. Quite clearly they will wish to have a different type of accommodation from single people, and what is a suitable variety of property at one point in time may be an unsuitable variety when the ratio of single people to married people has changed.

Changes in fashion and taste also affect property values. The effect is much more obvious in a market such as the clothes market;

at one point in time 15″ trouser bottoms may be in demand, a year or two later a fashion for 19″ may be in vogue, whilst a later change may be to bell-bottoms, before the whole cycle of change begins again. Fashion is important with property also, although in a less conspicuous way. Fashions change, as a study of older properties will reveal. Even though many pre-war houses provide good accommodation, the appearance of some is of doubtful quality. Often their unattractive design makes them difficult to sell, and many potential purchasers prefer to purchase a house of modern design and appearance, even though it may in other respects leave a lot to be desired. Many people want to be up-to-date with fashion and do not like to be left behind by others who have newer and more fashionable houses. Although the costly nature of property makes it difficult, if not impossible, for people to keep right up-to-date, changes in fashion over a period of years are evidenced in the price trends of different types of property.

Similarly, *the fashionableness of areas can change.* Chelsea is an outstanding example of a place which at one time was not particularly fashionable as a place in which to live, but later became so, with the consequence that the prices of its houses rose. Many humble cottages in Kensington have become the highly-priced homes of the affluent because it is fashionable to live in Kensington. Large sums have been spent on modernising and rebuilding them, and yet in many northern cities similar dwellings have been cleared by bulldozers because they were in areas which were not fashionable, and there were no affluent purchasers prepared to spend money on improving them. There may well have been other factors which led to this happening, but the fact that the areas were unfashionable doubtless helped to speed up the process of demolition.

Not only may an unfashionable area become fashionable, but unfashionable designs of property may also become fashionable. It may also happen that a type of property which is fashionable in one area, may be very unfashionable in other areas.

Changes in the type of society are important, but in the United Kingdom such changes are only likely to occur on a limited scale nowadays, as the major changes of this type took place in earlier times. The change from an agrarian society to an industrial society is probably the most obvious example, and to a limited extent this change is still taking place today in that people are still moving from jobs on the land to work in industrial areas. However, a reverse movement is also taking place, in that whereas in the past people moved out of the country to live in towns and their former homes were left empty and decaying, nowadays when the farm labourer moves from the country into industry to obtain higher wages his empty cottage is bought by a town dweller for conversion into a luxury country residence. This is another example of a change in society which results in changes in property values.

Changes in technology may also affect property values. In colder climates a house with central heating is invariably more valuable than a similar house which does not have central heating, but the difference in values has been decreased by the advent of improved installation techniques which enable complete central heating systems to be installed rapidly with a minimum of fuss and at relatively low cost.

Where factories are concerned, changes in technology may have far-reaching effects on values. It may be that new machines are designed and manufactured which carry out industrial processes more efficiently and more cheaply than existing machinery. If the new machinery is, however, taller than existing factory buildings, workshops with greater headroom will be required, and existing workshops may consequently become obsolete and less valuable.

Changes in building methods may affect property values. Improved building techniques will not necessarily result in changes in value; they may simply result in builders making higher profits if there is no increase in supply as a result of the implementation of the improved techniques. However, if the new techniques do result in an increased supply of new buildings to the market, unless there is an increased demand, or an increase in the money supply, the values or prices of that type of property should fall.

Similarly, *changes in building costs* may affect values if the result is that the supply of new properties to the market is also changed.

The *money supply* has already been mentioned in passing. If there is a change in the amount of money available for the purchase of property, without there being changes in any other supply and demand factors, this should result in changed prices in the property market. If more money becomes available for house-purchase, rivalry amongst potential purchasers may result in prices being bid up, whilst if there is a shortage of money the lack of purchasers with cash available may result in prices falling back. It should be noted that if there is an overall increase of money in the economy, any resultant price-changes may not represent changes of value in real terms, as the purchasing power of money may have fallen considerably where an increased supply of money is available to purchase only a fixed stock of goods.

Not only does the ease or difficulty of obtaining finance affect property prices, the *cost of such finance* is also very important. Even though plentiful funds may be available for property purchase, if the cost of borrowing is high potential purchasers may be deterred from entering the market. Borrowing £50,000 for house purchase at 8% per annum results in interest charges of £4,000 per annum, which may be well within the range of many people. However, if the interest rate increases to 16% a great many people would be unable to afford the increased interest charges which represent almost another £77 per week, every 1% increase in the cost of such a loan representing almost another £10 per week in funding costs. Changes in the cost of borrowing therefore affect property prices, as they affect the amount that potential purchasers can afford to borrow, although short term fluctuations are not likely to substantially affect the market. However, if for instance increases in the cost of borrowing are substantial and prolonged they may result in people "trading-down" from expensive to cheaper houses.

Proximity to good means of communication is a great advantage with virtually any property, and if there is any *improvement or deterioration in the means of communication* it is likely to have a marked effect on the value of properties which either benefit or suffer as a result of the change. Country cottages reasonably accessible to a motorway access or a main line railway station will usually fetch higher prices than those which are more remote, whilst with industrial and commercial properties the resultant price differences are likely to be even more marked. Few industrialists will wish to be too remote from their markets, particularly if transport costs form a large proportion of their overheads. Indeed, if the latter is the case, excessive transport costs could make their products uncompetitive in a competitive market. Employers of large working forces will benefit from good travel facilities in that the ease of travelling to work will make it simpler for them to recruit labour, and they may even be able to do so at lower wages than if they were situated in a location which involved employees in high travel costs. A study of property advertisements will readily reveal the emphasis placed on the existence of good means of communication, even with the humblest type of residence.

Planning control probably has a greater effect on property values than any other single factor, possibly even greater than all other factors combined. The power of the planner in today's world is very great indeed, and the decision of a planning committee can result in huge increases in value arising, or alternatively in such increases being denied. The farmer who obtains planning permission to develop his land as a residential or industrial estate may find that its value has increased fifty-fold as a result of obtaining the favourable decision. Had planning permission been refused, the value would have remained as for agricultural purposes with perhaps a slight incremental value reflecting the hope that permission might be obtained at some future date. Some of the big differentials in values to landowners which arise as a result of planning control will be diminished when gains arising from the existence of development value are taxed. Nevertheless, particularly where the potential purchaser is concerned, there will be a considerable difference in value in the market, dependent upon whether planning permission for a valuable use has been granted or not.

The above factors are some of the more obvious which may affect property values, but there will also be others which the reader will think of or encounter in practice. One of the essential items in the valuer's armoury should be an alertness to all the possibilities, with the resultant ability to detect the vital factors in a given situation.

CHAPTER 11

THE ROLE OF THE VALUER

What is the role of the valuer, and is it necessary to teach valuation? Statements to the effect that there is no need to consult a professional property valuer, and that old George who quietly sups his ale in the bar of the village pub knows as much about property values as anyone are often heard. Buy him a pint and he will tell you what prices different properties have fetched, what their advantages and disadvantages have been, and how properties currently on the market compare with these past sales. He may well be very good on local values, and with excellent local knowledge the advice which he gives may be first-class. In earlier chapters however, we considered many factors which should explain why old George will not always be a competent valuer. Firstly, properties come in all shapes and sizes, and although run-of-the-mill semi-detached houses (duplexes) may be easy for the competent amateur to value, others will be much more complex and may create valuation problems with which only the trained specialist can cope.

Legal complications can only be allowed for if a valuer has a good legal education. This may be necessary for him even to appreciate that a legal problem exists in some circumstances. Even simple legal factors can create problems for the valuer. Is a freehold or a leasehold interest to be valued? If a leasehold interest, what is the length of the unexpired term and how will a term of 35 years differ in value from a term of 28 years in a similar property? How large is the rent or ground rent payable under a lease? The higher the rent which has to be paid, the less valuable will be the leasehold interest, all other things being equal. What are the other rights and restrictions under the lease, apart from the length of the term and the level of rent? Is the tenant responsible for repairs, are there restrictions limiting the user of the property? Who pays the insurance premium? These and many other points will be important legal factors affecting value, and a layman would find it difficult, and in many cases impossible, to cope with such valuation problems.

Third parties may have legal rights over a property. There may be rights of way or rights of light owned by adjoining property owners, and such rights may restrict an owner's user of his property. Such rights may have a particularly adverse affect on value if redevelopment is under consideration and the most valuable scheme cannot be put into effect because of their existence.

Finding out about such rights is part of the job of the trained professional valuer. There was an instance a few years ago of a couple who purchased a new house on a new estate, only to have the local ramblers' association walk up the garden path and through their house. The ramblers were exercising rights along a footpath over which the house had been built. The trained valuer should be alert to such dangers, although it does not need a trained valuer to appreciate the drastic effect on value caused by such a state of affairs. This is an extreme example, but even the right of another person to share the use of a drive can have an adverse effect on a house, and the experienced valuer should be able to make a fairly accurate assessment of that effect in money terms.

Even where basically similar units exist side-by-side, the trained valuer with a good grounding in building methods and a knowledge of building costs can make accurate allowances for differences in the standards of finish and maintenance. How much difference in value does the existence of double-glazing, central heating or air-conditioning make, and what is the cost of installing such items? How much extra value results from the addition of a two-room extension, and what would be the cost of adding a similar extension to other properties? The layman with no knowledge of building costs or building technology would find it difficult to answer such questions.

Values will not necessarily vary proportionately with size, nor will they necessarily always vary by the same amount in respect of the presence or absence of such features as central-heating. This may not be such an indispensable feature in a warm locality as it would be in a cold locality, and it may be that only the trained valuer with his intimate knowledge of market conditions will be able to make an accurate allowance for the absence of a central heating system. Value is not necessarily related to cost, although a layman might sometimes be tempted to think it is.

Variations in values with changes in locality are sometimes quite astounding and the untrained man might often think some differentials to be so large as to be unrealistic and not factual. The trained valuer, however, is used to what may sometimes seem inexplicable market variations, and far from being puzzled by them he acknowledges them to be market facts for which he must make due allowance.

Whereas a layman may rapidly get out of his depth as far as values are concerned once he moves away from his own territory, a skilled valuer should be aware of the general factors which affect values and fairly rapidly be able to accustom himself to the tone of values in an area to which he is a stranger. He should be far-seeing and versatile enough to be able to value over fairly large geographical areas and should even be able to work from basic principles to value the type of property which rarely comes on to the market. The layman may be a good valuer with standard, uncomplicated properties in his own immediate locality, but the trained valuer should be competent with a wide range of properties over a wider area.

Liability for repairs has already been mentioned, and one of the skills of the valuer is to be able to assess the cost of outgoings arising from property ownership. How much does it cost to insure a property, and how is an insurance valuation made? What will it cost to paint and maintain cast-iron rainwater goods, and how will this compare with the costs for vinyl or aluminium rainwater goods? If a landlord supplies services for tenants, how much will these services cost? How much does it cost to provide central heating, hot-water, gardeners, hall porters and lifts?

These last few items are most likely to arise in the case of commercial properties, and it is with such properties that anyone but the skilled and experienced valuer is likely to find the greatest difficulty. Few commercial properties are even remotely similar to each other. Shops, offices, factories and warehouses are frequently built or adapted to the requirements of the current occupier. Only the skilled valuer will be able to make allowances accurately to reflect differences in properties of this type. He will be trained to know the effect on values of various features and will be closely in touch with the requirements of the users of such properties, and with the state of supply and demand in the market.

Where more specialised buildings are concerned only the trained valuer can hope to make a reasonable assessment of value. Public-houses, petrol-filling stations, cinemas, breweries, bottling-plants, sports-stadia and the like can only be valued by a person who knows just what affects the value of such properties. Such knowledge can only result from a good training and a thorough understanding of the market.

It seems to be a popular pastime nowadays to criticise the professional man and to decry his role, particularly by those least qualified to understand and therefore to criticise. As with all professions there is a whole range of skills amongst valuers and just as there are very good valuers there are also poor and even incompetent ones. In this respect the valuation profession is no different from any other but the fully skilled valuer has much to offer both individuals and society. No one else can provide his particular skill and expertise.

CHAPTER 12

RATES OF INTEREST AND YIELDS

The "yield" of an investment is a particularly important concept as it indicates to an investor the level of earnings of that investment, or the speed at which it will earn money. All other things being equal, the higher the yield the more attractive an investment will be. A 20% yielding investment will pay £20 per annum for every £100 invested, whereas with a 5% investment the return will only be £5 for every £100 invested. Thus, all other things being equal, the former would be the more attractive investment, but the concept of yields is a little more complicated, for a yield also gives an indication of the degree of risk attached to an investment.

Some investments will involve greater risk than others, and it is only natural that a higher return will have to be offered on riskier investments in order to tempt investors away from safer ones. Unless there is a possibility of a greater return a person is hardly likely to invest his savings in a risky venture, but if there is the prospect of a large pay-out this may persuade him that the risk is worth taking. This is not dissimilar from backing horses, in that the possible winnings from backing an odds-on winner are very much smaller, but more likely, than those which it is remotely possible to win by backing a 100–1 against horse which has little chance of winning.

In considering two investments an investor may also be influenced by the concept of what is known as "the pay-back period". With the 20% yield mentioned earlier £20 interest is received each year for an investment of £100. After five years the capital has been "paid-back", whereas with the 5% investment the capital would not have been paid back until 20 years had passed. This concept ignores the fact that annual earnings are an essential requirement from an investment. It is nevertheless a useful indicator as, with the riskier investment, the investor, having recouped his capital after five years can regard all future returns as the reward for his risk-taking. If there is a considerable risk attached to an investment he is likely to sleep better at night if the pay-back period is short. It is, of course, true that the shorter the pay-back period, the higher will be the yield. The incidence of tax on interest earned may lengthen the pay-back period.

In deciding what yield he is prepared to accept from an investment an investor will work on the basic principle that the greater the overall risk the higher will be the yield he requires. Conversely, as risks decrease he will be happy with lower yields, although it should never be forgotten that he will always hope to obtain the highest yield possible from any investment.

The yield which can be obtained will be affected by factors other than the risk directly attached to the actual investment under consideration. The attractions of alternative investments have already been discussed, and any prudent investor will always view the entire range of investment possibilities and make calculations to assist him to determine what course of action is best.

Before looking at the type of calculation which should be made it is necessary to explain the expression "nominal rate of interest". A company may decide to raise money to finance its activities, or to obtain capital from the market, as it is sometimes described. To do so it may decide to issue stock in £100 units at a nominal rate of interest which will depend upon the conditions in the money market at the time the stock is issued. This nominal rate of interest will have to be sufficiently high to persuade investors to part with their savings, otherwise the firm will not be successful in its efforts to raise capital. Not only will it have to be high enough to persuade investors that saving is more attractive than immediate expenditure, but it will have to be high enough to compete successfully with alternative forms of investment. Having considered these factors the company may decide that 10% per annum is the correct rate of interest at which to offer the stock, and each investor who purchases a unit of the stock will thereafter receive £10 per annum for every £100 of stock he purchased. This 10% will be the nominal rate of interest and the stock will be in units of £100 nominal value, but this does not mean that each stock unit will always be worth £100 or that the actual yield will always be 10%. Both the value of the stock and the yield may vary considerably with time and changing conditions in the financial market, and it may be that the only occasion on which the nominal rate of interest and the yield are the same is on the actual date of issue of the stock, (the date when it is first offered for sale).

The nominal rate at which stock is issued will usually be closely related to the minimum lending rate of the major banks at the date of issue. It is normal for governments to have a major influence in the important policy decisions of the "government bank" (that is the bank which is either under the direct control of the government or whose connections with the government are such that it is obliged to react to the wishes of the government of the day). Without such an arrangement it would be exceedingly difficult for any government to attempt to control economic conditions and to affect trends in an economy. As a result, the rate at which the government influenced bank or banks is prepared to lend money to a limited range of low-risk borrowers is an important financial indicator which reflects minimum lending rates in an economy to which all other lending and borrowing will tend to relate. In the United Kingdom the Bank of England has traditionally been the "government bank" in this respect and its Minimum Lending Rate has been the normal controlling factor in determining the cost of finance.

A few simple examples will be considered to show how nominal rates and yields work in practice.

Example 1
An inspection of the London Stock Market prices shows that on 8 July 1987, the following British Funds were listed.

					Int. only Yield %	Gross Redemption Yield
High	*Low*	*Stock*	*Price*	*+ or −*		
102⅛	95½	Treasury 12% 1987	100¾		11·9	9.064
134¾	120⅜	Treasury 14% 1988–01	129⅝	+ ¼	10·8	9.547
28¾	24⅜	Consols 2½%	27⅝		9·1	

The two left-hand columns give the highest and lowest market values at which a £100 nominal value unit of the particular stock stood during 1987. So the lowest market value of a unit of 2½% Consols during early 1987 was £24⅜ and the highest value of 12% Treasury Stock 1987 was £102⅛.

The "price" column indicates the value of the stock unit on the previous day, and the "+ or −" column shows whether this value represented an increase or decrease in value over the day before that.

The "Interest only yield %" column indicates the yield that an investor would obtain if he purchased the stock at the current price.

So with 2½% Consolidated Stock at a purchase price of £27⅝ an investor with £100 to invest could have purchased stock to a nominal value found by the following simple calculation:

$$\frac{\text{Amount to invest}}{\text{Purchase Price}} = \text{Units of stock bought}$$

$\dfrac{£100}{27\frac{5}{8}} = 3.6199$ units of £100 each or £361.99 nominal value of
stock.

The nominal rate of interest is $2\frac{1}{2}\%$ per annum, so in this instance
the yield on the investment can be found from the calculation,
Nominal value of stock held × nominal rate of interest = yield

$361.99 \times \dfrac{2.5}{100} = 9.05\%$ or 9.1% as printed to the first decimal
place.

Whereas the nominal rate of interest is only $2\frac{1}{2}\%$, because £100
of stock could be bought for only £27⅝ the actual yield was very
much higher. If the market value of the stock was above the
nominal value, then the yield would be below the nominal rate
of interest.

The column headed "Redemption" shows the yield which will
be obtained if the stock is bought at the current price and held
until it is redeemed by the borrower (until the borrower pays
back the original capital borrowed). When the nominal value
of the stock is repaid to the lender the stock is said to be repaid
at "par". Sometimes stock is repaid above par, which in effect
means that the holder of the stock at redemption date receives
the nominal value of the stock plus a bonus payment from the
borrower. So, if £100 stock units were repayable at 3 over par
the stock holder would receive £103 on the redemption date.
The receipt of the extra money results in the yield during the
period of ownership being increased slightly and the "redemption" column shows the yield calculated to include any redemption bonuses.

The possibility of the market value of a stock being above or
below the nominal value has been considered, so it will already
be apparent to the reader that stock prices fluctuate. A study
of the daily Stock Exchange list over a short period will soon
confirm this fact. Fluctuations in prices are nothing more than
the reaction of the price mechanism to supply and demand factors. If a stock suddenly becomes popular and investors wish
to buy it, its price will rise, whereas if its popularity wanes and
investors offer it for sale on the market then its price will fall,
unless there is an abundance of would be purchasers. The
operation of the market fixes the price of stocks and shares just
as with most other goods.

The reasons for a variation in supply or demand of a stock
or share may be many, but, whatever the reasons, a change
in price will also result in a change in the yield. As the price
of a stock rises so will the yield fall (unless the price rise is

balanced by a simultaneous increase in dividends paid on the stock). The more popular a stock becomes, the more its price is likely to rise and the yield to fall, and vice versa. Investors, in their eagerness to become owners of the stock, will bid up its price, and therefore a low yield is a reflection of the eagerness of investors to own a particular type of investment, whilst a high yield reflects their comparative lack of interest in a stock.

The relative regard of investors for stocks and shares can be seen from an inspection of the Stock Exchange prices, the following random selection of figures again being as at 8th July 1987.

High	Low		Price		+ or −	Yield	P/E
404	287	Trafalgar House Investments	400	403	+ 5½	4·6	15
280½	182	Marks and Spencers	253	255	− 1	2·4	25
224½	131	Amstrad	177	180	+ 1	0·3	18·8
298	187	Turner and Newall	296	298	+ 5	3·5	15·5
130	86	Leslie	92	102		29·9	

These few figures show a wide range of opinions, from investors who are willing to purchase Amstrad shares at a price which will only give a yield of 0·3% on their money, to those who will only purchase Leslie if they can get a 29·9% yield. The other three shares fall between these two extremes and give an indication of the wide range of yields which exist in the market at any point in time.

Two expressions which are frequently used in discussing shares are "price earnings ratio" and "asset value per share".

The price earnings ratio gives the relationship between the market price of a share and the annual earnings of the company which are attributable to that one share. So, if the total number of shares in a company are 1,000,000, its earnings are £225,000 and the market price is 247.5p, then the price earnings ratio is 11:1. Each share earns £225,000/1,000,000 or 22.5p, and its market price is eleven times the earnings. The P/E column in the above table shows price earnings ratios.

The asset value per share refers to the market value of the assets a company owns related to each individual share in the company. This should give an indication of the possibility of recouping investment funds if a company goes bankrupt. If the assets of the above company were considered to be worth £2 million on the open market, then the asset backing for each share would be £2. This suggests that anyone who buys a share at 247.5p could only lose 47.5p if the company became bankrupt and its assets had to be sold. Although this is a useful indicator of security, the investor should not place complete faith in it, as the value of the assets could well be subject to change or could be over-estimated.

To return to the concept of yields, these can be calculated at any point in time, and a calculation will show the return on an investment at that particular time. A similar calculation made at an earlier or later date may show a different yield resulting from changed circumstances, and although the actual annual return may remain constant, changes in capital values may result in there being a series of varying yields over a given period of time with any one investment.

Most property investors will be principally interested in what happens to their investment over a long period of time rather than what happens in the short term. Because of the time and cost involved, few people buy property with the intention of re-selling at an early date, and generally the intention is to retain it as a long-term investment. For this reason property investors will not be particularly worried about minor fluctuations in yields which may occur from time to time, as they will be primarily interested in what yield is obtained over the entire period of ownership of an investment. Indeed, they may even purchase investments on terms which apparently reveal a very poor yield, but calculations in retrospect a few years later may reveal that over the long term the yield has steadily improved and that the overall long-term yield is very favourable.

If yields are calculated monthly over a period of years it may be found that there are considerable fluctuations which throw up an uneven pattern of yields dependent upon underlying market conditions. Stock Exchange graphs showing performances of shares illustrate this point, both fluctuating capital values and fluctuating yields being revealed. In the stock market investors may well react to such fluctuations by immediately buying or selling if they think such a course of action advisable in the circumstances. Because the prime consideration of the property investor is the yield obtained over the lifetime of an investment, he will only take action if calculations reveal that the performance or likely performance of his investment over a relatively long period is such that positive action is required. It would, however, be pointless for him to react immediately to changes in investment yields, because before he could go through the necessary legal processes to effect a sale or purchase of a property interest, conditions might have reverted to their original state, and the reason for action would have disappeared.

The property market is consequently much less volatile than the stock market, and the general tendency is for slow and gradual change over periods of months or years rather than for violent and rapid changes from day to day.

In other respects the property market operates similarly to

the Stock Exchange in that prices result from the interaction of supply and demand. The general principles of yields are the same, with high yields being required for riskier property investments, and lower yields being acceptable from safer investments.

Over recent years there have been many variations in the yields applicable to various types of property, and there is little point in trying to suggest typical yields. Indeed, it could even be dangerous in view of the wide range of yields which might be found within even one particular category of property. However, a general indication will be given of the types of property which have found favour with investors in recent years, with suggestions as to the reasons for their popularity, and consideration will also be given to those types of property which have been unpopular.

Generally, the most popular types of property have been those which appear to offer security in real terms. These are usually well-built properties situated in the best type of location for their purpose and constructed to a modern design which will not restrict the potential user of the building, and which is not likely to become obsolescent at an early date. The quality of situation is all-important, as a valuable site will remain even when the buildings on it become unusable, whereas if the site is inferior the quality of the investment is likely to deteriorate rapidly as the buildings deteriorate.

Modern shops in prime positions have been much sought after by investors and have sold at low yields. The presence of a reputable tenant, such as a well-known national multiple trader, has been regarded as an added attraction, strengthening the security of income from the investment. Older properties and those in inferior positions have been less attractive, although an advantageous location has often been sufficient to outweight the disadvantages of an old building, particularly if modernisation and improvement can be effected without much trouble.

As the location of shops has become poorer, so has the willingness of investors to accept low yields decreased. The market for shops on the fringe of shopping centres, in neighbourhood centres and in poorer locations generally, has often been slack, with investors unwilling to put their funds into properties which are not in great demand by would-be occupiers, and in which there is little future potential. Investors have generally considered that demand will always be strong for prime position shops, but the changing shopping habits and modern marketing techniques will result in off-peak positions decreasing in importance.

The development of modern, self-contained shopping centres

with plentiful car parking space and facilities for refreshment and leisure, and the redevelopment and modernisation of older shopping centres to make more intensive use of existing shopping areas, have tended to centralise shopping activities more in recent years. The result has been that prime shopping locations have become even more valuable in relative terms, whilst locations remote from the new or redeveloped areas have become less attractive to both retailers and investors.

The comments concerning shops are almost equally applicable to offices. Modern office blocks in prime commercial situations have probably been even more attractive to investors over recent years than prime shops. Security in the long term seemed to be guaranteed if only because modern life, and government in particular, seems to revolve around an ever-increasing flow of paper and forms. There has therefore been a seemingly unending demand for well-located office buildings, especially those built to modern standards of design and possessing modern facilities. Well-located older blocks have also been popular, particularly if modernisation has been possible and feasible financially. The fear that the rapid development of modern telecommunication systems, which facilitate not only instant verbal contact but the incredibly rapid transfer of documents, would make central locations in major cities less essential and therefore less valuable in relative terms does not, as yet, appear to have become a reality. It will be interesting to monitor future trends as it may well be that the proximity of city centre office blocks to other city centre uses such as shops, theatres and transport systems may result in them remaining more in demand and more valuable than offices in other locations.

Factories and warehouses have generally changed hands at higher yields than offices and shops, largely because of the greater rate of wear and tear on such buildings and the greater risk of early obsolescence with changes in technology. Quality of situation has again been critical, and it is commonplace to see advertisements stressing that a factory is close to good means of communication or easily accessible to markets. Older, multi-storey factories, and industrial buildings in poor locations have been relatively unattractive to investors, as such units have limited appeal to industrial users and security of income is therefore low.

Residential properties in the United Kingdom have in the main been shunned by investors. For over half-a-century such properties have been subjected to a constant stream of legislation, much of which has decreased their attractiveness as investments by limiting the management powers of owners and restricting the rental income that such properties produce. Investors have consequently only shown much interest in those residences which have not been affected by such legislation, although the number of unaffected properties is rapidly becoming smaller. Because of the existence of burdensome legislation and controls, and the fear that they will increase rather than decrease, investors will only purchase residential property if the yield is high enough to compensate for the very considerable risks entailed.

In countries where residential investment properties have not been subject to the type of legislative control which has existed in the United Kingdom investors have in fact shown great interest in them. In Australia, for example, the purchase of a unit (a flat), or a duplex (a pair of semi-detached houses or bungalows) has been a popular way in which individuals have chosen to invest superannuation funds to provide a steady income flow on retirement. Market forces have been allowed to operate in fixing rental levels, and owners could get possession if properties were required for their own use or tenants proved unsatisfactory. The result of the lack of onerous controls was a substantial stock of residential properties available for rental, but the introduction in 1986 of legislation which is more onerous for investors resulted in the early withdrawal of accommodation from the rental market and a reduction in the appeal to investors of investment in residential accommodation. This early reaction in the market resulted in the government relaxing in 1987 some of the legislative provisions which had deterred investors.

For many years following the Second World War agricultural properties in the United Kingdom changed hands at incredibly low yields, in the region of 2% to 4%. There were several reasons for this, including the fact that agricultural products are a basic need of man and there will always be a demand for farms to produce them. Successive governments gave considerable aid to agriculture and this continuing policy doubtless strengthened the confidence of agricultural investors. There were for many years estate duty concessions on agricultural properties which increased their attractiveness as investments, although these concessions were curtailed on the advent of Capital Transfer Tax. Similarly, prospects of large gains resulted from the possible development of agricultural land. Such prospects were considerably reduced by the introduction of Development Gains Tax, and its successor Development Land Tax which in turn has been repealed. These factors, together with a period of low returns to agricultural production, resulted in yields on agricultural investments rising somewhat as market demand fell.

In the mid 1980's low returns to agricultural production have continued, whilst the decrease of government financial support and the imposition of controls by the European Economic Community have resulted in agricultural producers experiencing hard times compared to the previous 30–40 years, and a reduction in the attractiveness of agricultural properties as investments.

In other countries similar trends have been experienced, the relative unattractiveness of Australian agricultural properties in 1986–1987 resulting mainly from world gluts of wool and wheat with resultant low prices. The problems caused for Australian agriculturalists illustrates why for many years British Governments provided financial protection for farmers to protect them from world conditions beyond their control. The introduction and the removal of such assistance by governments can be of considerable importance in the property investment market as is also illustrated in the case of residential property.

Whatever the type of property, a wise investor will always work from basic principles in order to determine what is an acceptable yield and he will retain an open mind and have flexible investment policies to enable him to adapt to changing conditions in the market.

The future will inevitably see some property investments becoming more popular as others decrease in popularity. The student should endeavour to keep up-to-date with the underlying conditions of the property market so that he may not only be able to explain changes as they occur but hope to be able to predict them before they become reality.

CHAPTER 13

METHODS OF VALUATION

There are five conventional methods of valuation: the comparative method (or comparison), the contractor's method (or summation), the residual method (or the hypothetical development method), the profits method (or the accounts method or treasury method), and the investment method (or capitalisation).

The names in brackets are those used in different countries in lieu of the traditional English names for the methods, but the theory and practice remain the same wherever the methods are used.

THE COMPARATIVE METHOD
(Comparison)

This is probably the most widely used method and even if one of the other four methods is used by a valuer he will still almost inevitably have recourse to comparison as well. The method entails making a valuation by directly comparing the property under consideration with similar properties which have been sold, finding its value from these past transactions. Although this sounds simple and straightforward, there may be many pitfalls to trap the unwary. In using the method it is desirable that the comparison should be made with similar properties situated in the same area, and with transactions which have taken place in the recent past. The less the comparable property complies with these requirements, the less valid will be the comparison. Often a valuer is able to get evidence of sales which do accord with these requirements, particularly when a valuation is of a property such as a semi-detached suburban house (a duplex). However, the more uncommon a property is, and the more specialised the type of property, the less likely is it that the valuer will be able to find good "comparables", and it is not unusual for there to be a complete lack of evidence of sales of comparable properties.

Even when properties appear to be similar, close inspection often reveals that they are in fact different. A row of apparently identical houses may on internal inspection prove to have many differences, and the skill of the valuer will be required to make an allowance in money terms for such differences. Similarly, a skilled valuer will be able to quantify the difference in value caused by a different geographical situation.

It is essential in using this method to have as much evidence as possible readily available, and good office records are invaluable. Any valuer should ensure that he has an efficient filing system which is regularly kept up to date, and which contains as much information as can be obtained of each market transaction which is recorded.Modern computer filing systems greatly facilitate good record keeping and the almost instantaneous recall of information. However, for helpful records to be kept, there must be evidence of suitable comparables available, and unfortunately, in the real world, this is often lacking.

The word recent is a relative term. At some points in time a sale which took place a year earlier may be recent enough to be a valid comparison if the market has remained relatively stable in the intervening period. If the market has been volatile or has changed in any way during this time, then market evidence might need to be much more recent for it to be a good comparable. Even if there have been no transactions in the recent past, a valuer may be able to get some guidance from considering market evidence over a period of earlier years or months, as it is possible that a clearly defined trend of values might be detected. The valuer may decide that this trend would have continued through to the date on which he is making his valuation.

In using the comparative method a most thorough inspection of all the underlying factors in the market must be made in order to decide whether there have been changes in conditions since other transactions took place.

The method involves few dangers if the market is stable. When it is not stable, valuers may encounter problems in its use, and this may also be the case if there are few comparables, or if there are no true comparables, that is if the range of properties sold does not contain anything truly identical to the property under consideration.

Some differences may be relatively unimportant, and differences in architectural design, for example, may often make little difference to value. However, if a particular design renders a building inefficient in use, the difference may be very important, and in using the method the valuer should always consider such possibilities. The age of a building can be important in that it may be such as to render it either more or less fashionable and in many instances the structural condition and state of repair will be directly related to the age of the building. Valuers should also pay considerable attention to the accommodation offered by different properties, and try to make allowances for variations in the amount of floor space and differences in the lay-out and the number of rooms provided. Allowance should also be made for differences in the quality of fixtures and fittings, and for differences in the size of plots on which properties stand. Location is always very important, and valuers should be wary of assuming that values should be similar simply because the size and accommodation of properties is identical. A slightly different location can make a vast difference to market value.

In using this method the valuer should always bear in mind the fact that property is heterogenous, and should always ask himself whether any special factors affected the market value of the comparables that he is using, or whether any special factors are likely to affect the value of the property which he is considering.

The following is an example of the comparative method in use.

Example 1

A valuer has to value a four-bedroom house which provides net usable space of $180\,m^2$. His research reveals that in the same street there have been sales of similar sized four-bedroom properties as follows:

> 12 months ago a house of $180\,m^2$ sold for £90,000
> 8 months ago a house of $170\,m^2$ sold for £86,700
> 6 months ago a house of $185\,m^2$ sold for £95,275
> 3 months ago a house of $175\,m^2$ sold for £91,500
> 1 month ago a house of $185\,m^2$ sold for £97,600

After analysing these sales he decides that whereas the first sale revealed a capital figure of £500 per m^2 of usable space, the last sale was at a figure of £527.50 per m^2 of usable space. The valuer also notices there has been a consistent rate of increase of £2.50/m^2 per month in the capital values of this style of house and he therefore values the subject property at £95,400 ($180\,m^2$ @ £530/m^2).

This is a very simple example of the comparative method in use and in reality its use will normally be more complicated. It would be necessary to check whether the various houses provided similar numbers of rooms in total, whether their locations were of equivalent quality, whether their fixtures and fittings were similar and of equal quality, and also to check on other features of each of the properties. Adjustments in the analysis of each piece of market evidence would be necessary to allow for variations in such factors, and it is likely to be rare in the real world that market analysis and use of the analysed information would be as straightforward as in the example above.

There is a great danger in the use of comparable evidence that the valuer may place too much faith in it, forgetting that whilst such evidence reflects what happened in the past his present task is to determine what the current value of property is. Current market value may be affected by different factors to those which affected past transactions and it could therefore be that past evidence might be of only very limited assistance or in extreme circumstances it might be positively misleading.

However, in spite of the need for great care in the use of the comparative method and the frequent shortage of suitable comparable evidence, it is a method which the valuer will use regularly and which will give reliable results if used properly and in the correct circumstances.

THE CONTRACTOR'S METHOD
(Summation)

This is used to value the type of properties which seldom change hands and for which there are therefore few comparables. It must at this point be stressed that cost and value are rarely the same, but this method of valuation is based loosely on the assumption that they are related. It should therefore be appreciated that it is a method used only infrequently, and which is something of a last resort. The basic theory of the contractor's method is that the cost of the site plus the cost of the buildings will give the value of the land and buildings as one unit.

With the majority of properties there is ample evidence to show that this proposition is not correct, but the contractor's method is used to value properties for which there is little general market demand and which are consequently rarely sold. The types of property for which it could be appropriate are hospitals, town halls, schools, libraries, police stations, and other such buildings. It will be noted that this list comprises principally public buildings, although the use of the method is not necessarily restricted to public buildings alone. Cost is normally only one factor of many which may affect supply and demand and which therefore affect value, but it is probably true that with this type of building it is a predominant factor. It would always be possible for the would-be users of such buildings to acquire alternative sites and to construct new buildings rather than purchase an existing property at a greater overall cost. Competition between rival potential users would be unlikely and it is therefore reasonable to assume that cost and value are not unrelated with such specialist buildings.

However, if an alternative building were constructed it would be a new property, whereas with an existing property it is obvious that there would be some wear and tear resulting from its previous use and there might also be a degree of obsolescence which had arisen since it was new. In using the contractor's method the valuer must therefore make a deduction to allow for both depreciation of the buildings and obsolescence of design. The basic valuation approach then becomes as below:

	Cost of Site
Plus	Cost of Building
Less	Depreciation Allowance and Obsolescence Allowance
	Value of Existing Property

This method is most frequently used for rating purposes where rates are levied on the value of buildings and sites together and it is also sometimes used in valuations for compensation when property of a specialist nature has been compulsorily acquired.

The following illustrates the typical use of the Contractor's method of valuation.

Example 2

A public library which occupies a site on the fringe of a town centre has to be valued. The building is about 100 years old, built in a rather ornate style and shows some evidence of deterioration.

The valuer using evidence and his own judgement decides that an equivalent site would today cost £800,000, that a 500 m² building in the same style would cost £1,250/m² to build today, and that considerable allowances should be made for deterioration and obsolescence. He accordingly values as follows:

		£
	Cost of Site	800,000
Plus	Building cost 500 m² @ £1,250/m²	625,000
		1,425,000
Less	25% obsolescence allowance (based on building cost)	156,250
		1,268,750

Less   15% depreciation allowance   93,750

Value of existing property £1,175,000

Expressed as a hypothetical example in a book, the method appears simple to use. In reality all the inputs to such a valuation are likely to be difficult to determine, even the building costs which will be far from clear-cut in the case of the unusual types of building for which the method is used. In particular, the precise allowances to be made for depreciation and obsolescence are very difficult to determine and very much dependent upon the judgement of the individual valuer.

THE RESIDUAL METHOD
(Hypothetical Development Method)

This is used when a property has development or redevelopment potential. It is needed when there is an element of latent value which can be released by the expenditure of money on a property. Residual valuations are quite regularly made by people who purchase residential properties which they consider could be made more valuable if money were spent on improvement and modernisation. This would-be purchaser may look at a house and decide that it is worth £50,000 and that it needs expenditure of a further £20,000, after which it will have a market value of £90,000. A quick inspection of the figures shows that latent value of £20,000 has been released by the expenditure on improvements. This is a very simple example of the method in use, but even when much more complicated calculations are involved, the basic approach to the method is still exactly the same.

	Value of the completed development
less	Total expenditure on improvements or development (including developer's profit)

Value of site or property in its present condition
(Residual Value)

The value of the completed development is sometimes referred to as the Gross Development Value, or as the Gross Realisation.

The use of the residual method involves considerable skill and it is first necessary to decide what is the best form of development suitable for a site or property, and then to predict the value of such a development after it has been completed. This is not an easy task, as apart from the skill involved in choosing the best use for a site, the valuer also has to estimate the value of a building which does not as yet exist. He has to cast his mind forward to some future date and imagine the building in existence on the site before he can begin to estimate the Gross Development Value.

Even when this has been done with great skill and accuracy, all the costs of improvement and development must then be estimated. These may include such items as the cost of site clearance, architects' fees, site engineer's fees, quantity surveyor's fees, and all other professional fees incurred in creating the development. The costs of building must be estimated, and these could well increase during the time-lag between the acquisition of the property and the completion of the development. Once a property has been developed it has to be let or sold, and the valuer must make an allowance for all costs which would be incurred in letting or disposing of the property he envisages as one day standing on the site. These costs will include estate agents' fees, advertising fees, and the solicitor's fees and legal expenses. To purchase the site and subsequently develop or redevelop it will usually require a considerable amount of finance, and the costs of obtaining this must be deducted as a development cost. No one will wish to take all the risks involved in a project without any reward, and a developer's profit must be allowed.

There may be other items of expense to consider, and the more variables there are the more difficult it will be to maintain an acceptable degree of accuracy in the calculations. However, a skilled valuer with a specialist knowledge of the type of development for which he is valuing, who is in touch with the market and who is familiar with the costs of development, can use this method with a considerable degree of accuracy.

There will doubtless be instances in which, in retrospect, a purchaser will be seen to have paid too much for a property because the figures on which the residual valuation was based have changed in the period since the property was purchased. The method is nevertheless acceptable for finding market value, as it must always be remembered that this value is the figure which would be paid in the market at a definite point in time; taking into account future expectations. It is not unusual in any aspect of life for retrospective consideration to show that an earlier decision was based on false assumptions, and the fact that a residual value may subsequently be shown to have been optimistically calculated does not alter the fact that in the light of circumstances at the time of purchase the estimate of market values was correct.

The method is often criticised as being clumsy and containing too many variables, but there is little doubt that it is the only real method of valuation applicable when there is latent value in a property.

The following simple example illustrates the way the method is used in practice.

Example 3

A site with approval for the development of four houses of $160\,m^2$ each is to be auctioned and a developer wishes to know how much he can afford to bid for it. He estimates it will take one year to complete and sell the development, that he will have to pay 16% per annum interest on borrowed money, and that the houses will cost £400/m^2 to building including all site works and the provision of services. He also decides that he will require a profit of £15,000 per house, each house having an anticipated market value of £115,000.

His residual valuation is as follows:

Four detached houses at £115,000 each
Gross Development Value £460,000

Less	Costs of Development:		
(1)	Building costs: 4 houses × 160 m² @ £400/m²	= £256,000	
(2)	Professional fees (Architect's, planner's, quantity surveyor's) @ 10% of building costs	= 25,600	
(3)	Cost of borrowing half of (1) + (2)		
	@ $16\% = \dfrac{16}{100} \times \dfrac{281,600}{2}$	= 22,528	
(4)	Legal expenses on sale of houses say	12,000	
(5)	Agent's fees on sale of houses say	8,000	
(6)	Advertising costs on sale say	1,000	
(7)	Developer's profit = 4 × £15,000	60,000	

Total development costs £385,128

Residual Sum .... £ 74,872

On the above calculations the developer considers the sum of £74,872 is available to cover the purchase price of the land, all the expenses he will incur on the land purchase, and the interest charges he will incur on holding the land from the date of purchase until the development scheme is completed and sold. He will calculate these costs and his bid price for the land will be reduced below £74,872 by the amount of these costs.

All the costs he uses in this valuation will be carefully assessed by the valuer in an effort to calculate a realistic figure for the land value. However, because they are all predicted figures the accuracy of the valuation will depend upon the skill and judgement of the valuer.

The selling price of the houses will be based on his market knowledge, whilst items (1) and (2) will be based on his knowledge of costs and perhaps even on the preliminary estimates of builders and professional advisers.

Until the development is built and sold the developer will incur the cost of interest on money borrowed to complete the development, or alternatively he will sacrifice interest earnings if he uses his own money. As a general rule, a realistic estimate of the amount of money a developer will need on average throughout the development period is half the cost of building and half the cost of professional fees, as calculated at (3). Clearly, such a calculation is only an approximation of interest charges, but it is nevertheless a useful approach for initial development appraisals.

Items (4), (5) and (6) are costs which are likely to arise with any development and the valuer will assess them on the basis of recent experience of such costs.

The developer's profit is the return for his expertise and the reward for the risks he takes, and there is no fixed rule for the calculation of this figure. It is sometimes calculated as a percentage of Gross Development Value, sometimes as a percentage of Building Costs, or it may be calculated by other methods thought appropriate by individual developers, such as the profit per house used in the above example.

The residual sum found is based on the anticipated sale of the completed development at a future date, in the above example twelve months time. If the developer bids for the land he must therefore allow for the professional fees and legal costs he will incur on purchasing the land, and also on the interest charges he will incur during the development period on borrowing the money for the land purchase and the associated costs.

The above example is relatively simple, but even complex residual valuations are only developments on this basic approach.

THE PROFITS METHOD
(Accounts Method, Treasury Method)

This is based on the assumption that the value of some properties will be related to the profits which can be made from their use. The method is not used where it is possible to value by means of comparison, and is generally only used where there is some degree of monopoly attached to a property. Such a monopoly may be either legal or factual, a legal monopoly existing where some legal restraint exists to prevent competition to the property user from the users of other property. Such a situation may occur when a licence is required for the pursuit of a particular trade. A factual monopoly may arise when there is some factor, other than a legal restraint, which restricts competition. An instance of a factual monopoly is the restaurant at the top of Mount Snowdon in Wales where there is no other property to offer competition and where none is likely to be built. Whenever there is an element of monopoly it is obviously not possible to use the comparative method of valuation, as there could be no true comparison to a property which enjoys a monopoly, and it is also a reasonable assumption that any rent which would be paid for the use of such a property would relate to the earning power in that use. It should be noted that with this method the valuer attempts to estimate the rental value of a property and not the capital value. Profits are made on an annual basis, and any figure obtained from them will also be on an annual basis. The basic equation on which the profits method is based is as follows:

	Gross Earnings
less	Purchases
	Gross Profit
less	Working Expenses (Except Rent)
	Net Profit

Part of the net profit which the business earns must be allocated to pay the tenant for his work in the business, a further allocation must be made to cover his risk and enterprise, and a final allocation to allow interest on the capital he has put into the business. Care should be taken that a deduction for the tenant's wages has not previously been made in calculating the net profit, as double counting must be avoided. After allowance has been made for these various items, a sum of money will remain which would be available to pay for the use of the premises. This figure will vary, depending upon the size of the deductions for other items, and skill is required, and a knowledge of trading returns, for a valuer to be able to make a reasonable assessment of the division of net profit between these various items.

Much care is also needed in the calculation of the net profit and in the use of the various figures involved. If a business is already in existence there will be accounts which can be inspected. The obvious approach is to base a valuation on those accounts. However, care is necessary, as a business may have been badly run and the use of the accounts figures in such circumstances would give too low a net profit. Alternatively, a business may have been run by an exceptional, astute and hard working business man, and no other trader might be able to achieve the same level of profits. In such circumstances no other trader might be prepared to pay the same level of rent, whilst in any case the super-efficient trader would require a large share of the profits for himself as a reward for his skill and management. If such a situation does exist, the valuer should not take too high a proportion of the net profits as rent, as he is only endeavouring to assess what normal market value is, not what a property may be worth to a super-efficient business man. It also sometimes happens that accounts do not give a true reflection of trade, either because they have been badly kept through ignorance or inefficiency, or because the business man has chosen not to put all items through his books.

In practice the method is normally used in the valuation of hotels, and public houses and sometimes for cinemas and theatres. It is regularly used in rating valuation, the annual value which is obtained being directly related to the value required for rating purposes. In other instances a valuer may have to convert the annual figure into a capital figure. This will be done by means of the investment method, which is the fifth conventional method of valuation.

The following is an example of how the method might be used in practice.

Example 4

A valuer has to assess the rental value of a restaurant which has a licence for the sale of alcoholic drinks and which took £179,000 in the last trading year. He inspects the books and decides the business has been run in a way other potential tenants would run it, and he produces the following valuation.

Gross takings £179,000

Less Purchases £47,600
        Running expenses 59,700
                                                                         _____
                                                                              107,300
                                                                         _____
                                                                               71,700

Less Owner's remuneration £20,000
        Interest on capital (furniture, kitchen
        fittings, etc.) @ 12% on £37,000 4,400
                                                                         _____
                                                                               24,440
                                                                         _____

                      Divisible balance .... £ 47,260
                                                                         ===========

Using his judgement the valuer decides the divisible balance
would be split 55% profit to business, 45% available for rental;
therefore estimating the rental value to be approximately £21,000
per annum.

THE INVESTMENT METHOD
(Capitalisation)

This is based on the principle that annual values and capital
values are related to each other and that, given the income a
property produces, or its annual value, the capital value can
be found. The method is widely used by valuers when properties
which produce an income-flow are sold to purchasers who are
buying them for investment purposes.

Many properties are let to tenants and the income they produce
is known. In other cases, although a property may not be let,
it is possible to predict what its rental value is by comparing
it with similar properties which have been let. If this is the case,
or if a rent actually passes on a property, the only problem the
valuer faces is determining the relationship of annual value to
capital value. The way in which the conversion is made is by
the use of a multiplier which is commonly known as "Years'
Purchase", or, in abbreviated form, the "Y.P." As will be seen
later, in valuation terms, this multiplier is more appropriately
described as the Present Value of £1 Per Annum.

The Years' Purchase or multiplier is derived from the rate of
interest which an investor decides he will require from a property, that is, the yield which he wishes to obtain. This yield
reflects the quality of the investment in comparison with other

property investments, and other investments generally. Consideration has been given to factors which may influence the investor in his choice of yield, and the valuer will obviously need to be conversant with these when using the investment method. Here again an element of comparison arises, as the valuer will be comparing both other investments and properties. The choice of the yield, and its conversion into a suitable multiplier will be considered at length in Chapter 15.

In addition to these conventional methods, valuations can be made using *Discounted Cash Flow* techniques. These are to all intents and purposes extensions of the Investment Method, and entail estimating all future items of income which an investment will produce, and converting these future sums into present day equivalents in money terms. These future cash flows will be the sums remaining after taking account of anticipated future outgoings, so that only the net income for each future period will be discounted back to its present value. Calculations are usually based on periods of one year. When the present value of the net income for each year has been calculated, the total of all the discounted figures will represent the present capital value of the investment.

There are several different types of approach to discounted cash flow calculations, but generally they all amount to a more comprehensive form of investment valuation, with more variables being included in the calculations and with each year's income assessed separately. As very versatile and cheap calculating machines are now available, the objection that such techniques involve too much complicated mathematics is no longer valid. The quality of the results which emerge from the calculations will, however, depend to a very large extent on the quality of the inputs, that is, the figures which are estimated for future returns and outgoings, and the rates of interest used for discounting.

The techniques will be considered further in Chapter 19.

THE MORTGAGE/EQUITY APPROACH

As the majority of property purchasers have to raise finance by borrowing, the investment method of valuation in its simplest form may not provide an entirely correct way of assessing the value of an interest. What can be termed a *mortgage/equity approach* should really be adopted, giving a basic calculation as in the following example.

Example 5   Total Property Income £ 20,000 p.a.

| Purchaser's Capital | £100,000 |
| Return required 11% | ·11 |

Purchaser's Income Requirement   £ 11,000

Balance available to pay mortgage interest   £ 9,000 p.a.

Mortgage obtainable @ 14% per annum

Interest payable = Mortgage Capital × Interest rate

$$£9,000 = \frac{MC \times 14}{100} \qquad MC = £64,285.70$$

| | Equity | £100,000 |
| *Plus* | Mortgage | £ 64,285 |

Maximum price payable for property   £164,285

The annual income being known, the potential purchaser first calculates the return required to his own money (his equity), and deducts this from the income to leave a balance which is available to pay interest on any money borrowed on mortgage.

As the interest rate charged on mortgage money will be known, he is then able to calculate how much mortgage capital can be borrowed for that amount of annual interest, and this is the second calculation.

The maximum he can then afford to pay for the property is the sum of his own money and the money he can afford to borrow. If he pays more than this sum he will have to borrow more money, his mortgage interest charge will increase, and the return to his own capital will then be too low. If he can purchase the property for less than this sum he will get a better return on his own capital.

This approach will be considered again in a later chapter.

CHAPTER 14

VALUATION TABLES

Valuing property is partly an art and partly a mathematical process. The mathematical content of most valuation work is relatively limited and quite straightforward, and there is no reason for any newcomers to the subject to fear that they may be unable to cope with the mathematics. There is nothing magical or mysterious about the concepts employed, and this is also true of valuation tables.

In the United Kingdom the most commonly used tables are "Parry's Valuation and Conversion Tables", published by The Estates Gazette*, which are produced simply with the intention of making a valuer's life easier. They are one of the tools of the trade and, as with a handyman's tools, they help to take the drudgery out of jobs and enable them to be done more rapidly. They do not provide valuation answers in themselves; they merely provide rapid answers to many of the mathematical calculations which a valuer may have to make. Ownership of a set of tables does not make one into a competent valuer.

Practically every calculation made by a valuer involves compound interest theory, and the valuation tables are a series of compound interest tables with what can be described as variations around the basic compound interest theme. This basic theme is that when money is invested the original capital sum earns interest which, if it is added to this capital, will in subsequent years itself earn interest. This process will be repeated each year, and the capital is therefore regularly increased and, as a result, the interest earned increases with each period, or it compounds.

This basic theory is used in a number of different tables, each of which will be considered and the practical implications explained. It must be stressed that in the following pages the author uses only sufficient mathematics to give a basic understanding of the tables. Because of this emphasis on the minimum of mathematics those who wish to become more involved with this aspect should refer to either "Parry's Valuation Tables" or "Modern Methods of Valuation".

* All references in this book are to the Tenth Edition of the Tables.

There are other sets of valuation tables in use besides Parry's. These include Rose's Property Valuation Tables, Donaldson's Investment Tables and Bowcock's Property Valuation Tables. Which set of tables is used will depend to some extent on the preferences of the valuer and to some extent on the purposes of the valuation. Each set is constructed using slightly different variations on the basic compound interest theme, and answers obtained after using the different tables will therefore vary slightly. The valuer should take care that he understands the underlying principles in the construction of each table that he uses to ensure that his valuation is based on the correct assumptions and the correct mathematical process.

There are also numerous cheap and versatile electronic calculators on the market, and those who are proficient at mathematics can in fact dispense with the use of valuation tables. Some of the more advanced calculators are programmed to give equivalent calculations to those provided by valuation tables, and it is therefore a matter of choice for the individual valuer as to whether he uses a particular set of tables or relies upon an electronic calculator.

The reader should note carefully that all the examples which follow have been done using the Tenth Edition of Parry's Valuation Tables.

Readers from countries in which the £ is not the unit of currency can substitute their own country's currency in the remainder of this chapter, e.g. the Amount of $1, the Present Value of $1, etc.

The Amount of £1 Table

This table shows the amount to which £1 will accumulate if it earns a given rate of compound interest for a given number of years.

The student should note carefully that there is a single investment of £1 only which is invested to earn compound interest. The amount of £1 will always be greater than unity, as each figure will represent the original capital plus compound interest earned. It follows that the total interest earned is the figure found in the appropriate column of the tables, less the £1 originally invested.

The calculations on which the tables are based are as follows:

	Capital at start of year	*Interest earned during year*	*Capital at end of year after interest has been added*
Year 1	£1	i	$1 + i$
Year 2	$1 + i$	$(1 + i)i$	$(1 + i) + (1 + i)i$ or $(1 + i)^2$

Year 3	$(1 + i)^2$	$(1 + i)^2 \times i$	$(1 + i)^2 + [(1 + i)^2 \times i]$ or $(1 + i)^3$
Year 4	$(1 + i)^3$	$(1 + i)^3 \times i$	$(1 + i)^4$
"N" years			$(1 + i)^N$

N = the number of years
i = interest earned by £1 in 1 year

The concept of "i" sometimes causes confusion with students, but it is really quite simple. If the rate of interest is 5% per annum, £100 will earn £5 in one year. £1 would therefore earn £5/100, or 5p. Expressed in decimal form this is £·05.

A simple calculation can be done to show how the above calculations work when a specific rate of interest is chosen.

	Capital at Start of Year £	Interest at 10% £	Capital at end of Year £
Year 1	£1	·10	= 1·1
Year 2	1·1	$(1.1) \cdot 1 = \cdot11$	1·1 + ·11 = 1·21
Year 3	1·21	$(1.21) \cdot 1 = \cdot121$	1·21 + ·121 = 1·331
Year 4	1·331	$(1.331) \cdot 1 = \cdot1331$	1·331 + ·1331 = 1·4641

So the amount of £1 in 4 years at 10% is 1·4641, but instead of doing the above calculations this figure could be rapidly looked up on page 100 of Parry's Tables. The figure tells us that if £1 is invested to earn interest at 10% and it remains undisturbed for 4 years, at the end of that period there will be a total fund of £1·4641, representing the original £1 and £0·4641 accumulated interest.

It is interesting to consider a few figures in this table to understand fully the effect of the compounding of interest, and to see how rapidly the rate of accumulation increases as the time or the rate of interest increases.

			Total Interest earned by £1
Amount of £1 @ 2% in	3 years = 1·0612		£0·0612
	10 years = 1·2190		£0·2190
	20 years = 1·4859		£0·4859
	50 years = 2·6916		£1·6916
Amount of £1 @ 10% in	3 years = 1·3310		£0·3310
	10 years = 2·5937		£1·5937
	20 years = 6·7275		£5·7275
	50 years = 117·3909		£116·3909
Amount of £1 @ 20% in	3 years = 1·7280		£0·7280
	10 years = 6·1917		£5·1917
	20 years = 38·3376		£37·3376
	50 years = 9,100·4381		£9,099·4381

The figures need little explaining, but it is interesting to note that at 10% almost as much interest is earned in 10 years as is earned in 50 years at 2%. The 20% figures illustrate the almost staggering interest accumulations at high rates over a long period of time, and make one ponder what a marvellous old age could be enjoyed by a prudent youngster lucky enough to find a 20% investment.

The use of the table can best be explained by an example.

Example 1

If £1,200 is deposited and is left undisturbed for 17 years, earning interest at 6%, what sum will be available at the end of the time period.

Sum deposited	£1,200
Amount of £1 in 17 years at 6%	2·6928
(page 98 of Parry's Tables)	
Sum available after 17 years	£3,231·36

The calculation is based on the simple proposition that if £1 becomes a certain amount after a given period of time at a given rate of interest, larger deposits will accumulate to larger amounts in direct proportion to their relationship to a £1 deposit.

To summarise and to stress the important facts,

(1) The Amount of £1 Table gives the basis for the other valuation tables.
(2) The Amount of £1 Table is based on compound interest calculations.
(3) Amount of £1 figures are always greater than unity.
(4) The excess over unity represents total interest earned.
(5) The formula for calculating the amount of £1 is $(1 + i)^n$ where "i" is the interest earned by £1 in 1 year, and "n" is the number of years.
(6) The amount of £1 is often referred to by use of the symbol A, e.g. $A = (1 + i)^n$.

The Present Value of £1 Table

The Present Value of £1 Table gives "the sum which needs to be invested at the present time at a given rate of interest in order to accumulate to £1 by the end of a given period of time".

Alternatively it can be defined as "The present value of the right to receive the sum of £1 at a given time in the future, discounted at a given rate of interest".

The two definitions together explain the concept of the present value of £1 or "V", as it is frequently written. A person who has the right to receive £1 at some future date would be as well off were he to receive a lesser sum now which could be invested to earn sufficient interest to ensure that, by the time the future date was reached, that sum plus the interest earned would be equal to £1. The opportunity cost concept is involved, as anyone who had the right to receive £1 at a future date would only sell that right for a figure which left him no worse off financially today.

The figures found in this table again involve capital figures of £1 and are based on compound interest calculations. They are the reciprocals of those found in the Amount of £1 Table, as if £1 invested today will amount to $(1 + i)^n$ at a future date, the right to receive £1 at a future date must be worth $1 \div (1 + i)^n$ or $1 \div A$.

An inspection of a few typical figures from the tables may again prove interesting.

Present Value of £1 in 3 years @ 2% = £·9423223
                       10 years @ 2% = £·8203483
                       20 years @ 2% = £·6729713
                       50 years @ 2% = £·3715279

                        3 years @ 10% = £·7513148
                       10 years @ 10% = £·3855433
                       20 years @ 10% = £·1486436
                       50 years @ 10% = £·0085186

                        3 years @ 20% = £·5787037
                       10 years @ 20% = £·1615056
                       20 years @ 20% = £·0260841
                       50 years @ 20% = £·0001099

These figures illustrate how the present value of the right to receive £1 at a future date decreases the more distant that date is, and they show how this decrease is even more marked at high rates of interest. They also illustrate how much more highly the future is valued when the opportunity cost rate of interest is low. Where this is 2%, £1 in 50 years' time is today worth over 37p, but where it is 20%, £1 in 50 years' time is today worth about 1/100 of one penny.

Again, the use of the table in practice is best illustrated by examples.

Example 2

An investor has the right to receive £20,000 in 10 years' time. What sum would he be prepared to accept today in lieu of that future sum?

It is found on enquiry that money can today be invested to earn interest at the rate of 8% over the next 10 years.

Sum receivable in 10 years' time	£20,000
× Present Value of £1 in 10 years at 8%	.4631935
Present value of £20,000 in 10 years at 8%	£ 9,263·87

This calculation suggests that the investor will be as well off accepting £9,263·87 today as if he waited 10 years for the £20,000. The validity of the assumption can be checked by calculating what figure will be available in 10 years' time if he does in fact invest the money today.

Example 3

Sum available to invest	£ 9,263.87
× Amount of £1 in 10 years at 8%	2·1589
Total available after 10 years	£19,999·768

There is a small error revealed in the checking which could be avoided if more decimal places were used. The example illustrates both a common use of the Present Value of £1 Table, and also its relationship with the Amount of £1 Table as shown in the checking.

Example 4

A sum of £8,750 must be available in 12 years' time to meet expenditure which will be essential at that time. What sum should be put aside today to meet this future expense if 7% interest could be earned in the intervening period?

Sum required in 12 years' time	£8,750
× PV £1 in 12 years at 7%	·4440120
Sum to be invested today	£3,885·105

The reader can obtain practice in the use of the tables by carrying out a check similar to that in the previous example.

To summarise, some of the important facts relating to this table are:

(1) The table is based on compound interest calculations.
(2) The present value of £1 is the reciprocal of the amount of £1.
(3) The present value of £1 is always less than unity.

(4) The formula for calculating the present value of £1 is

$$V = \frac{1}{(1 + i)^n} \text{ or } V = \frac{1}{A}.$$

(5) The difference between any given present value of £1 and unity represents the interest that could be earned by that present value of £1 if it were invested for that period and at that rate of interest.

The Amount of £1 Per Annum Table

This table gives the amount to which a series of payments of £1 invested annually at the end of each year will accumulate over a given period of years if compound interest is earned at a given rate.

The Amount of £1 Table involves a single payment of £1, but quite frequently money is saved or spent at regular intervals of time. The Amount of £1 Per Annum Table envisages a series of payments of £1 at the end of each year, each £1 going into an ever-increasing fund on which compound interest is earned.

It should be carefully noted that the payments are made at the end of each year, and this is almost the same as if the first payment were made a day later, that is at the beginning of the second year. If the concept of the Amount of £1 Per Annum is considered in this way any figure could be found by taking the Amount of £1 figures at the appropriate rate of interest for a time period of one year less than the required time period, adding them together, and then adding a further sum of £1 to the total representing the £1 deposited on the last day of the time period.

For a time period of 5 years at 10% the Amount of £1 Per Annum could be found by adding the figures in the table on page 87, and adding a further £1 for the last year, giving a total of 6·1051.

Alternatively, whenever the amount of £1 per annum is required, the following calculation could be made, but it is far easier to find the answer in Parry's Tables, and this particular figure can be found on page 118.

End of Year	Capital saved	Period for which interest is earned	Accumulates to	Total at end of 5th year
1	£1	4 years	A£1 in 4 yrs @ 10% =	1·4641
2	£1	3 years	A£1 in 3 yrs @ 10% =	1·3310

3	£1	2 years	A£1 in 2 yrs @ 10% =	1·2100
4	£1	1 year	A£1 in 1 yr @ 10% =	1·1000
5	£1	No interest as paid		£1·000
		into fund on last day		
		of the 5 years		—
	Amount of £1 Per Annum in 5 years @ 10%			6·1051

It will be noted from the above calculations that the result comprises a total of capital invested of £5 (£1 for each year of the period considered) plus total accumulated interest of £1·1051.

It was noted in the Amount of £1 Table that when long periods and high rates of interest were involved, the resultant figures were surprisingly high. With the Amount of £1 Per Annum Table in similar circumstances the results are even more surprising, and it is useful to consider a few figures from the table.

			Total Capital	Total Interest Earned
Amount of £1 p.a. @	2% for	3 yrs	3·0604	3	·0604
	2% for	10	10·9497	10	·9497
	2% for	20	24·2974	20	4·2974
	2% for	50	84·5794	50	34·5794
	10% for	3	3·3100	3	·3100
	10% for	10	15·9374	10	5·9374
	10% for	20	57·2750	20	37·2750
	10% for	50	1163·9085	50	1113·9085
	20% for	3	3.64	3	·64
	20% for	10	25·9585	10	15·9585
	20% for	20	186·688	20	166·688
	20% for	50	45497·19	50	45447·19

The 20% figures cannot be found in Parry's Tables, but are shown above for consistency with previous examples. Some of the figures are almost unbelievable but they are mathematical facts and they clearly illustrate the rewards for regular saving, particularly if high rates of interest can be earned.

The formula for calculating the amount of £1 per annum is $\dfrac{A-1}{i}$ where A = the amount of £1 and i is the interest earned by £1 in 1 year. It can be written more fully as $\dfrac{(1+i)^n - 1}{i}$. For those who have difficulty remembering formulae, it may be helpful to remember that in this table the figures are large, and the denominator i, being small, will help to give appropriately large results.

As before, the use of the table is best explained by examples.

Example 5

A man of strong will and frugal habits manages to save £1,000 per annum out of his salary. He invests this at the end of each year to earn interest at 7·5%. What sum will he have available at the end of 18 years?

Annual savings	£1,000
Amount of £1 per annum at 7½% for 18 years	35·6774
Total available after 18 years	£35,677·4

The total capital invested is 18 × £1,000 or £18,000, and the balance of £17,677·4 is accumulated interest.

Example 6

Woodland has been planted which will take 40 years to mature, and it is estimated that £4,800 per annum will have to be spent on maintenance. What will the true cost of maintenance have been when the timber reaches maturity, if the woodland owner has to borrow capital at 11%?

Annual maintenance cost	£4,800
Amount of £1 per annum over 40 years at 11%	581·8261
	£2,792,765·2

The actual capital spent will be 40 years × £4,800 or £192,000, and the balance of £2,600,765·2 represents the interest which would be payable on the money borrowed.

Alternatively, if the owner had not needed to borrow money the £2,600,765·2 would represent earning power he had sacrificed by investing his money in trees.

In summary, some important features of the Amount of £1 Per Annum Table are:

(1) The table concerns a series of annual payments of £1.
(2) Each payment is made at the end of the year, the first payment being at the end of the first year.
(3) The table is based on compound interest calculations.
(4) The last payment earns no interest.

(5) The formula is $\dfrac{A-1}{i}$ or $\dfrac{(1+i)^n-1}{i}$

The Annual Sinking Fund Table

This table gives the amount which must be invested annually at the end of each year to provide £1 at the end of a given period, taking into account the accumulation of compound interest at a given rate during the period concerned.

As the sum which finally accumulates is only £1, each of the annual sums will be considerably less than £1, and the longer the time over which the money accumulates and the higher the rate at which interest is earned, the smaller will be the size of the annual instalments. A sinking fund is nothing more than a savings fund into which a series of equal annual payments are made with the object of ensuring that a specific sum of money is saved by a given future date. At that future date the fund will comprise all the annual payments that have been made into it plus the compound interest earned by each annual payment since the date it was first put into the fund.

An inspection of some of the figures will illustrate some of these points, and will give the student some idea of the type of figures involved.

Annual Sinking Fund to redeem £1 in	3 years @ 2%	·3267547
	10 years @ 2%	·0913265
	20 years @ 2%	·0411567
	50 years @ 2%	·0118232
Annual Sinking Fund to redeem £1 in	3 years @ 10%	·3021148
	10 years @ 10%	·0627454
	20 years @ 10%	·0174596
	50 years @ 10%	·0008592
Annual Sinking Fund to redeem £1 in	3 years @ 20%	·2747252
	10 years @ 20%	·038523
	20 years @ 20%	·0053565
	50 years @ 20%	·0000219

These figures need little explanation and it is apparent that only very small amounts need to be saved annually if the fund is to accumulate over a long period, particularly if high rates of interest are involved. If it is remembered, for instance, that £·02 is 2p, it will be realised just how small a figure £.0000219 is. However, it is extremely doubtful if anyone would ever be fortunate enough to get such a favourable rate of interest as 20% for a sinking fund.

A building society mortgage is in practice somewhat similar to a sinking fund in that a mortgagor borrows a sum of money and then makes a series of equal payments over a period of time at regular intervals to ensure that at the end of the time sufficient money has accumulated to repay the debt. The essential requirements and the operation of a building society mortgage are similar to those of a sinking fund, although the student should be warned that the concepts behind the mortgage calculations are different, even if the mathematics involved gives the same result in money terms.

The Annual Sinking Fund is proportional to the Amount of £1 Per Annum. With the latter table a series of annual payments of £1 are made to accumulate to a larger future sum. With the Annual Sinking Fund a series of proportionately smaller payments are made to accumulate eventually to £1. So the Annual Sinking Fund formula is the reciprocal of the Amount of £1 Per Annum formula, that is:

$$\text{Annual Sinking Fund (ASF)} = \frac{1}{\text{Amt £1 p.a.}} \text{ or } \frac{i}{A-1}$$

As with previous tables its use in practice will be illustrated by means of examples.

Example 7

£20,000 will be required to purchase a new car in 10 years' time. Money can be invested today to earn interest at $7\frac{1}{2}\%$ in the intervening period. What amount should be invested annually at the end of each year to ensure that sufficient money is available in 10 years' time?

Annual Sinking Fund to accumulate to £1 in 10 years at $7\frac{1}{2}\%$ (page 87 of Parry's Tables)	·0706859
Total capital required	£20,000
Total Annual payment required	£1,413·718

The total annual payment is merely a multiple of the figure found in the tables in the ratio that the sum eventually required relates to £1.

Example 8

The validity of the above calculation can be checked by use of the Amount of £1 Per Annum Table.

Amount to which £1 per annum will accumulate in 10 years at $7\frac{1}{2}\%$	£14·1471
Annual savings	£1,413·718

Amount to which £1,413·718 saved
annually for 10 years will accumulate,
interest being earned at 7½%   £20,000·009

This proves that the Annual Sinking Fund will fulfil its objective, and it also illustrates its relationship to the amount of £1 per annum.

Example 7 involves ten annual payments each of £1,413·718. At the end of the ten years the £20,000 available will comprise 10 × £1,413·718 or £14,137·18 of capital saved, plus accumulated compound interest amounting to £5,862·82.

In the property world this table is extremely useful if it is known that capital sums will be required at future dates, and there is a regular income, such as rents coming in, from which ASF payments can be made. The replacement of fixed equipment in buildings, the renewal of roofs, re-pointing and similar jobs could all be allowed for by setting up Annual Sinking Funds.

In summary, the more important features of the Annual Sinking Fund are:

(1) The table concerns a series of annual savings each less than £1.
(2) The sum eventually saved is £1.
(3) The £1 saved comprises all the annual capital savings plus accumulated compound interest.
(4) The last year's savings earn no interest, being placed in the fund on the last day of the last year.
(5) The ASF formula is $\text{ASF} = \dfrac{1}{\text{Amt £1 p.a.}}$ or $\dfrac{i}{A - 1}$.

The Present Value of £1 Per Annum

This table shows the present value of the right to receive an annual income of £1 at the end of each year for a given number of years, each year's income being discounted at a given rate of compound interest.

It is possible to find the value of such an income-flow from the Present Value of £1 Table, and if an income of £1 were receivable for each of the next 6 years it could be valued as follows, the value of each £1 receivable being the PV of £1 for the number of years preceding the receipt of that £1.

PV of £1 in 1 year @ 8% = ·9259259
2 years @ 8% = ·8573388
3 years @ 8% = ·7938322

$$4 \text{ years } @ 8\% = \cdot7350299$$
$$5 \text{ years } @ 8\% = \cdot6805832$$
$$6 \text{ years } @ 8\% = \cdot6301696$$

Present Value of the right to
receive an income of £1 per annum
for 6 years discounted at 8%
(PV of £1 Per Annum for 6 years at 8%)   £4·6228796

The present value of £1 per annum for any period at any rate of interest could be found simply by adding the figures from the Present Value of £1 Table for each of the years involved. With long periods this would soon become very tedious, and the Present Value of £1 Per Annum Table obviates the need for such a time-consuming exercise. The £4·6228796 found above can be looked up direct on page 34 of Parry's Tables where it is rounded off to 4·6229, but although it is therefore not necessary to refer to the Present Value of £1 Table it is nevertheless important to remember its relevance.

As with previous tables, an inspection of some of the figures from Parry's Tables may be helpful.

Present value of £1 per annum in 10 years @ 2%	8·9826
20 years @ 2%	16·3514
50 years @ 2%	31·4236
Perpetuity @ 2%	50·0000
10 years @ 10%	6·1446
20 years @ 10%	8·5136
50 years @ 10%	9·9148
Perpetuity @ 10%	10·0000
10 years @ 20%	4·1925
20 years @ 20%	4·8696
50 years @ 20%	4·9995
Perpetuity @ 20%	5·0000

It is apparent from the above that when low rates of interest are involved the present value of £1 per annum figure for any period is relatively high, and that where high rates of interest are involved the figure is relatively low.

If the reader refers back to these figures after completing this chapter he will note that when an income-flow in perpetuity is valued at 2%, 32·7% of the total capital value is attributable to the first 20 years' income-flow, when 10% is used 85% of the total capital value is attributable to the first 20 years' income-flow, whilst when 20% is used almost 84% of the total value is attributable to the first 10 years' income-flow. In the latter instance nearly all the value is attributed to the near future, and it is well to remember at this stage that 4·1925 represents the sum of the PV's of £1 at 20% for each of the first 10 years.

In the earlier calculation the right to receive £1 per annum for 6 years was considered. The right to receive any larger sum for the same period discounted at the same rate would be proportionately larger and the use of the table can be illustrated by example.

Example 9
What is the present value of the right to receive an annual income of £375·50 at the end of each of the next 6 years, discounted at 8%?

Annual Income	£ 375·50
Present Value of £1 Per Annum for	
6 years at 8%	4·6228796
Present Value of the right to receive	
£375·50 for 6 years at 8%	£1,735·8912

Example 10
What is the value of an annual income of £6,875 for the next 27 years discounted at 7%?

Annual Income	£ 6,875
PV of £1 p.a. for 27 years at 7%	
(Page 32 of Parry's Tables)	11·9867
Capital value of income of £6,875	
for 27 years at 7%	£82,408·562

Example 11
What is the value of an annual income of £1,000 receivable in perpetuity at 9%?

Annual Income	£ 1,000
PV of £1 p.a. in perpetuity at 9%	
(Page 35 of Parry's Tables)	11·1111
Capital value	£11,111·1

The last three examples are in fact simple valuations using the investment method of valuation, annual income-flows having been converted to capital figures by means of multipliers.

The present value of £1 per annum is the best title for this multiplier as it explains what it represents, but it is more commonly referred to as the years' purchase, or YP for short.

The reader will note that in Example 11 the income is receivable in perpetuity, that is there is no future date at which the income-flow will cease, but that it will continue permanently. As in all other instances the YP is the addition of each PV of £1 for each of the years the income is receivable. Mathematically the figure can be found from the formula:

PV of £1 per annum in perpetuity or YP in perpetuity

$$= \frac{100}{R} \text{ or } \frac{1}{i} \text{ where R = rate of interest \% and i}$$

= the interest earned by £1 in 1 year.

The validity of this formula can be checked by examples.

Example 12
What is the value of an annual income of £750 receivable in perpetuity discounted at 4%?

Annual Income	£750
YP in perp. @ 4% = $\frac{100}{R} = \frac{100}{4} =$	25
(Page 31 of Parry's Tables)	
Capital Value	£18,750

If the above-income flow is purchased for £18,750 we can check whether the YP has converted income into a capital value in the right ratio to ensure the correct return on the money invested. A 4% return is required on £18,750

$$\frac{18,750 \times 4}{100} = £750, \text{ and the YP has fulfilled its function correctly.}$$

Example 13
What is the value of an income of £20,000 per annum receivable in perpetuity, being the rent from a good-class shop? The appropriate rate of interest is 7%.

Rental Income   £20,000

YP in perpetuity @ 7% = $\dfrac{1}{\cdot07}$ 14·285714

(Page 33 Parry's Tables—14.2857)
                                                            £285,714·28

The functioning of the YP can again be checked, a 7% return on capital being required.

$$\frac{285{,}714{\cdot}28 \times 7}{100} = 19{,}999{\cdot}999$$

As the property produces £20,000 each year it can be seen that a 7% yield is in fact obtained if £285,714·28 is paid for it, and that the YP in perpetuity has correctly fulfilled the task of converting annual income into a capital value.

The use of the PV of £1 per annum table or the YP will be considered again in the next chapter, which deals with the Investment Method of valuation, and a summary of the more important features of this table is:

(1) The table concerns a series of annual receipts of £1 each.
(2) Each £1 is received at the end of the year.
(3) The receipt of each future £1 is discounted at an appropriate rate of compound interest.
(4) The formula for the Present Value of £1 Per Annum in Perpetuity is 100/R or 1/i (the formula for the YP for a limited period will be considered in a later chapter).
(5) The function of a YP is to show the relationship between income and capital, and to convert income-flows into capital values.

The Tables—General
It will have been noticed that all the above discussion relates to interest calculations which are made annually, and to receipts and payments at specific times, for example at the end of each year.

The formulae can be adapted to allow for variations in the pattern and it would be relatively simple for a YP to be worked out on the basis of each £1 being received at the beginning of each year, which is probably more practical in the modern world, in which rent is invariably payable in advance. However, the current set of Parry's Tables is based on the descriptions as above.

If interest calculations are necessary at intervals of less than one year, it is possible to work out the correct figure by adaptation of the Amount of £1 formula, which is $A = (1 + i)^n$. If "t" is the number of interest calculations made in any year, the formula $A = (1 + i/t)^{tn}$ will give the correct Amount of £1. So if interest calculations are made half-yearly the formula becomes $A = (1 + i/2)^{2n}$ and if monthly calculations are made it becomes $A = (1 + i/12)^{12n}$. The meaning of "i" and "n" in the formula remains as before. As A is the basis of all the other formulae, by use of this adapted formula any of the other tables can be calculated for interest periods of less than one year. Although such adjustments will not always give absolutely correct answers, the resultant figures will be sufficiently accurate for most valuation purposes.

CHAPTER 15

THE INVESTMENT METHOD
OF VALUATION
(CAPITALISATION)

This method has already been discussed briefly, and the purpose of this chapter is to look a little deeper into its use in practice, and to consider the role of the Years' Purchase.

As stated earlier, the method involves the conversion of an income-flow from property into an appropriate capital sum. The income-flow can be actual or notional, the former occurring when a property is let on lease and the tenant pays a rent for use and occupation. There is a notional income-flow when an owner occupies a property himself, as although he will obviously not pay a rent, the notional rent is the figure which he would otherwise have to pay to acquire the use of a similar property. The value of the property to him as an occupier should also be at least as great as the market rental value, otherwise he would be better off letting it on the market. So, even if property is not let, the full rental value can be estimated, and this is also possible when a property is vacant and available to let. The investment method of valuation can therefore be used even when no rent actually passes on a property.

The *full rental value* of a property is the maximum rent for which it could be let in the open market on a given set of letting terms. The concept envisages that it is possible to let the property at that rent, and it follows that if the full rental value is known a valuer can use it in his valuation, confident in the knowledge that it would be paid by at least one potential tenant. The assessment of full rental value requires a thorough market knowledge, and skill in the application of that knowledge on the part of the valuer. The more onerous the terms on which a property is offered the lower will be the full rental value, and vice versa. If a property is offered on the condition that a tenant would be responsible for doing all repairs, the full rental value would be lower because of the extra responsibility for repairs. If the terms on which a property is to be let are varied, there will normally be a complementary variation in the full market rent.

The assessment of a full rental value will invariably involve comparison with similar properties which have recently been let. In many circumstances direct comparison may not be possible because of the differences in size of different properties, and the valuer will frequently have to rely upon the use of *Units of Comparison*. If a factory of 1,000 m² has to be let and there is evidence of lettings on three factories of 700 m², 900 m² and 1,200 m², the valuer would reduce each piece of market evidence to a price per square metre, a square metre being the unit of comparison. He would study the property to be valued and the three comparables, and would choose a suitable price per m² for his valuation. In choosing a figure he would make any adjustments he considered necessary to reflect differences between the various properties, such as differences in quality of accommodation and location, and possibly even to reflect the existence in the market of a quantity allowance. (See later.)

The essential feature of units of comparison is that properties of varying sizes are reduced to a common unit of area to enable comparison to be made between them. Typical units of comparison are listed below, both metric and imperial units being quoted

	Units of Comparison	
	Imperial	*Metric*
Building Land	Per acre	Per hectare
	Per square yard	Per square metre
Residential Building Land	As above and also per unit of accommodation or per plot.	
Factories and Warehouses	Per square foot	Per square metre
Offices	Per square foot	Per square metre
Shops	Per square foot	Per square metre
	Also in some instances per foot or per metre of shopping frontage to the street.	
Agricultural Land	Per acre	Per hectare
Fishing rights	Per rod, or per foot or yard of river bank	Per rod or per metre of river bank
Cinemas and Theatres	Per seat or per full house	

There is no rule that says the above have to be used, and customs vary in different areas. As long as the valuer is consistent in his choice of unit a valid comparison can be made.

The actual *assessment of rent* is an important process, as any discrepancy at this stage will be multiplied many times once a multiplier is used to convert the rent to capital value. This is not to suggest that complete accuracy is possible in assessing rental values, as the best that can be hoped for is a reasonably accurate and intelligent estimate, the valuer's own judgment being as critical a factor as the mathematical analysis. The process of comparison and assessment of rental value will be illustrated by a number of examples.

Example 1

A single-storey shop with a frontage of 6 m and a depth of 13 m has to be let. What rent is it likely to command if a near-by single storey shop with a frontage of 5 m and a depth of 13 m was recently let for £10,000 per annum?

Analysis of recent letting
5×13 @ £10,000 per annum = 65 m² @ £10,000
$= £153 \cdot 8462/m²$

Rent assessment
6 m × 13 m @ £153·8462/m² = Estimated rental value
$= £12,000$ per annum

Alternative analysis
5 m frontage @ £10,000 per annum
$= £2,000/m$ frontage per annum

Rental assessment
6 m frontage @ £2,000/m frontage = £12,000 per annum.

Note. Analysis by means of value per metre frontage can only be done if properties are of similar depth. When different depths are involved a process known as "zoning" is normally utilised (see later).

Example 2

A site of 2·5 hectares with planning permission for 65 semi-detached houses has recently been sold for £195,000. Another near-by site of 1·8 hectares with planning permission for 54 semi-detached houses has to be valued for sale.

Analysis of sale
2·5 hectares @ £585,000 = £234,000 per hectare
or
65 units @ £585,000 = £9,000 per house plot

Density $= \dfrac{65}{2 \cdot 5} = 26$ plots per hectare

Valuation
The valuer will first note that the density is somewhat greater on the land to be valued.

54 units on 1·8 hectares $= \dfrac{54}{1 \cdot 8}$ plots per hectare

$= 30$ plots per hectare

In view of the greater density the houses, when completed, will probably sell for less. The valuer may therefore decide that each plot is worth £8,500.

Value of 1·8 hectare site = 54 units @ £8,500 each = £459,000.

Note. Although this valuation utilises a lower price for each plot, the total site value is greater than if a valuation had been made using the unit of comparison "price per hectare". The latter unit would not have allowed for either the greater density of development or the lower value per plot. An adjustment could have been made to it in an attempt to allow for these two factors, but such adjustments are much easier when applied to the smaller unit of comparison of the single plot.

Example 3

A factory of 2,000 m² has to be valued for rental purposes. It is similar to three other factories of 2,200 m², 1,800 m² and 1,500 m², each of which was recently let for £52,800, £48,600 and £42,750 per annum respectively.

Analysis of comparables
1. 2,200 m² @ £52,800 per annum = £24/m²
2. 1,800 m² @ £48,600 per annum = £27/m²
3. 1,500 m² @ £42,750 per annum = £28·5/m²

It is apparent that the rental value per m² decreases as the size of the factory increases. Such a trend sometimes occurs in the market, but this is not always the case. The valuer should take care to ascertain that such variations do not arise because of other factors, before he makes a "quantity allowance".

"Quantity allowances" may occur if for no other reason than that the management costs per m² may be lower on a large area than on a smaller one, and the freeholder may therefore be prepared to accept a lower average rent. They do not always occur, and their existence will generally depend upon a number of supply and demand factors.

Valuation
In this case the valuer may decide that £25·5/m² is an appropriate value.

2,000 m² @ £255/m² per annum.
Rental value = £51,000 per annum.

"*Zoning*" was referred to earlier, and is a technique which is sometimes used to enable a rather more sophisticated comparison to be made between units of varying sizes. It is used principally with shops, as the area immediately adjacent to the street is generally more valuable than the space at the rear of the shop. The space at the front of a shop can be used for display purposes to attract passing pedestrians, and enticing the customers inside a shop is perhaps the most important step in promoting a sale. The area behind this can be utilised for sales purposes, whilst that at the rear of the shop is possibly only usable for storage. It is therefore common for shop rents to be "zoned", the front zone having the highest value, the next zone a lower value and subsequent zones even lower values. The depth of a zone and the decrease in value between zones are not fixed by any rigid rules, but are arbitrarily fixed as a result of market negotiations between landlords and tenants. However, it is often found that zones have been calculated at 20 feet depths, and are now calculated at 7 metre depths. It is rare to use more than three zones in valuing or analysing transactions. It is generally found that values are "halved back" with zoning, for example Zone A (the front zone) at $£X/m^2$, Zone B at $£X/2/m^2$ and Zone C at $£X/4/m^2$.

Example

72, High Street, a shop with 7 m frontage and 18 m depth, was recently let for £16,500 per annum. The rental value of 68, High Street, which has a frontage of 5·3 m and a depth of 16 m, is required.

72 HIGH STREET £16,500 per annum		*68 HIGH STREET*	
7 m		5·3 m	
ZONE A	7 m	ZONE A	7 m
ZONE B	7 m	ZONE B	7 m
ZONE C	4 m	ZONE C	2 m

Analysis of 72, High Street

Zone A = 7 m × 7 m @ £X/m^2 =   49X

Zone B = 7 m × 7 m @ £$\frac{X}{2}$/m^2 =   24·5X

Zone C = 7 m × 4 m @ £$\frac{X}{4}$/m^2 =   7X

Total Rental Value £16,500 per annum =   80·5X

£204·97 = X

The value/m^2 of Zone A = £204·97
The value/m^2 of Zone B = £102·48
The value/m^2 of Zone C =   £51·24

These figures would not have been used in practice to find the rental value originally, and figures of £204, £102 and £51 were probably used. However, for comparison with No. 68 it is best to be consistent and to use the figures as analysed.

Valuation of 68, High Street. On the assumption that in all respects other than size the properties are truly comparable, the rental valuation is:

Zone A = 5·3 m × 7 m @ £204·97 =   7,604·39
Zone B = 5·3 m × 7 m @ £102·48 =   3,802·01
Zone C = 5·3 m × 2 m @   £51·24 =   543·14

Full Rental Value   = £11,949·54

In practice this would probably be rounded off to £12,000 per annum.

For a further study of zoning the student should refer to "Principles and Practice of Rating Valuation" published by The Estates Gazette.

Once a rental has been estimated or is known, it must be reduced to a figure of *net income* before it can be converted into a capital value. An investor can only spend the money which remains after he has paid all the outgoings for which he is responsible, and any liabilities must be deducted from the gross rental to give the net rental value.

Outgoings which a landlord may have to pay include repairs, insurance premiums, general rates, water rates, general services charge, and management costs.

Repairing liabilities may vary considerably from property to property and from lease to lease. It is common for a lessor to attempt to make a lessee take on all the repairing liabilities. If this happens the landlord will generally have to spend nothing on repairs, but the valuer should always be prepared to make a contingency allowance for repairs if it appears that a tenant may be financially unable to meet his repairing commitments, or if he appears to be the sort who may disappear at dead of night, leaving expensive repairs to be done. If the lessor is liable for repairs, his liability may vary from being responsible for structural repairs only, or for external repairs and structural repairs, to being responsible for all repairs. The valuer should carefully determine the extent of the liability by examining the lease documents, and he should then inspect the property and carefully estimate the cost of complying with any repairing liability. The anticipated repairs should be costed, and it is not acceptable to allow a percentage of the rent to cover repairs. The rent passing on a property does not necessarily give any indication of likely repairing costs which will be related to the situation and exposure of a building, the local climate, the design of the building, the materials of which it is constructed, the quality of past maintenance and the degree of wear and tear involved in its current usage.

The cost of *insurance* against fire and similar risks will be related to the cost of constructing a similar alternative building. As insurance is an indemnity against loss, the valuer must estimate the cost of replacing the present building in the event of its being destroyed. As with repairs, this is not necessarily related to the rent produced by a property, and insurance costs should not be estimated by taking a percentage of the rent. The area of the building must be calculated, the cost of constructing a building of that size must then be worked out, and the premium charged by the insurers will be directly related to that cost, and will be the figure to be deducted as an outgoing.

Rates, both *general and water and the general service charge*, are normally the liability of an occupier, and will not often have to be paid by a landlord. When they are his liability, the amount payable will be the Rateable Value of the property multiplied by the Rate in the pound for the area in which the property is located.

Management expenses will occur with virtually all property interests, even when the landlord has no repairing liabilities, and no other responsibilities. In the latter circumstances the landlord will still have to check that the tenant is complying with all his obligations, and he may also have expenses connected with collecting and banking the rent and keeping accounts. When the landlord does the management himself the cost will be his out-of-pocket expenses and the cost of his time. When managing agents are employed the cost will be their charges, which will be related to the work and expense involved, and which may be levied on the basis of a percentage of the rent passing on the property.

Once the net income has been calculated the capital value will be proportional to it in a ratio which will depend upon the quality of the property as an investment. As discussed earlier, this will be revealed by the yield, or the rate of interest at which it is valued, which will have been determined following comparison with alternative investments.

To illustrate how the market operates, a number of hypothetical, but not untypical, transactions will be considered.

1	2	3	4
Property	*Net Income*	*Capital Value*	*Multiplier*
Factory	£15,000	£135,000	9
Factory	£16,500	£150,000	9·09
Factory	£67,500	£615,000	9·11
Shop	£7,500	£93,000	12·4
Shop	£10,500	£130,000	12·38
Shop	£13,500	£170,000	12·59
Offices	£45,000	£650,000	14·44
Offices	£120,000	£1,700,000	14·17

Column 2 shows the rents being produced by the properties listed in column 1, whilst column 3 shows the prices for which these investments have been sold. Column 4 has been calculated from columns 2 and 3 and shows the relationship that each sale-price bears to the income the property produces. It can be seen that although all the multipliers are different, there is a reasonable consistency between similar classes of property, with factories being capitalised with a multiplier of approximately 9·1, shops with about 12·5, and offices with just over 14. The consistency of multipliers within a particular class of property is not always as regular as that illustrated, but it is a market fact that within one class of similar quality properties, the multipliers evidenced by sales are reasonably consistent. The variation between 9 and 14·44 in the table above reflects the different regard of investors for the different types of property, and indicates that offices are most favourably regarded as investments, whilst factories are least favourably regarded. In valuation terms the figures reveal that property investment valuations were done on a basis which approximates to the following pattern:

Factories	*Shops*	*Offices*
Net Income	Net Income	Net Income
×9	×12·4	×14·3
————	————	————
Capital Value	*Capital Value*	*Capital Value*

Our consideration of these transactions is in retrospect, but the investors who purchased the properties would have decided the figures they were willing to pay by doing valuations similar to the above. They would have chosen a rate of interest which they considered would give them a yield which adequately reflected the risks involved, and from this rate the Years' Purchase would then have been calculated. This basic approach is used in most investment valuations, although the calculations may become more complex when there are variations in the income-flow over time, or when terminable incomes are involved.

If the figures in the table are considered further they can be related to the formula for the Years' Purchase in Perpetuity which is $YP = 100/R$. With the first factory this becomes $9 = 100/R$ and R must therefore be $11 \cdot 1$. This indicates that this factory was considered to be a good investment if the income it produced was an $11 \cdot 1\%$ return on capital.

The price of the first shop can be analysed in a similar way, the Years' Purchase being $12 \cdot 4$, $YP = 100/R$ becomes $12 \cdot 4 = 100/R$, and R must therefore be $8 \cdot 06$. This indicates that the purchaser of the freehold considered it to be a good investment if he received an $8 \cdot 06\%$ return on his capital.

The reader may care to calculate the yields on each of the other properties.

It can be seen from the table that the lower the yield an investor is prepared to accept, the higher will be the multiplier with which he will capitalise the income-flow. It follows that if two investors are interested in one property, the investor who is prepared to accept the lowest yield will place the highest capital value on the property, and vice versa.

Another aspect of this fact is that the poorer the investment is, the higher will be the yield the investor will require, the smaller will be the Years' Purchase and the lower the capital value which results. The converse also applies.

When called upon to value other offices, shops and factories, the valuer who possesses the market evidence in the table will be influenced by it. If a property similar to one of these classes of property has to be valued, it will be reasonable for him to expect it to be valued on a similar basis and at a similar rate, unless he has good cause to suspect that investors have changed their investment criteria.

As the investment method involves capitalising an income-flow, a valuer might be tempted to think that if that income is known, a visit to a property to inspect it is unnecessary. This is not the case, and an inspection should always be made, as it is otherwise impossible to tell whether the income-flow can be expected to increase or decrease in the future. The quality of the property must be ascertained for this purpose and also to determine the correct yield and to estimate any outgoings which may have to be met. No matter how small the income-flow or how humble the property, an inspection should always be made.

At this stage it may prove helpful to read again the section in Chapter fourteen dealing with the Present Value of £1 per Annum, or Years' Purchase. A reconsideration of the mathematical concept and the examples which show how the Years' Purchase fulfils its role may be useful.

The *analysis* of market evidence involves nothing more than valuation in reverse. The capital value or rental value is known, and analysis is an attempt to find out how such figures were originally calculated. The unknown will usually be either the rental value or the yield at which the property was valued. It is rather like attempting to reconstruct a crime, and it is almost inevitable that, when analysing, a valuer will have to make certain assumptions and deductions. In doing so he must exercise as much skill as possible, but there will nevertheless be an element of doubt in most analyses. It is consequently dangerous to suggest that the results of analysis necessarily prove anything; at best they suggest what probably happened in a given situation.

The simplest way to analyse transactions is to adopt exactly the same approach as in valuing, and to use the symbol "x" for the unknown quantity. Some simple analyses are illustrated in the following examples.

Example 5

The freehold of a shop which is let at the full rental value of £9,000 per annum was recently sold for £75,000. A valuer with a similar shop to value wishes to find the yield on this comparable.

Full Rental Value	£9,000 p.a.
Years' Purchase in Perpetuity	x
Capital Value	£75,000

$$9,000x = 75,000 \qquad\qquad x = 8\cdot3333$$

The Years' Purchase in Perpetuity $= 8\cdot3333 = \dfrac{100}{R}$

The rate of interest with which the property was valued is therefore 12%.

Example 6

A freehold factory which was recently let at full rental value has just been sold for £1,350,000. A similar factory has to be valued, and the valuer wishes to use this market evidence. The factory has 5,900 m² of usable floor space.

Full Rental Value	x
Adopt a Years' Purchase	
calculated at 11% in perpetuity	9·09
Capital Value	£1,350,000

$$9·09\,x = 1,350,000 \qquad\qquad x = £148,515$$

The full rental value as calculated is £148,515 per annum, which represents a rent of approximately £25·17/m².

It will be noted that to do this analysis the valuer had to assume a yield of 11% as there were two unknowns, the full rental value and the yield. In adopting a yield he will have utilised his knowledge of the investment market for industrial properties, and the rate chosen is therefore a considered estimate rather than a guess. Obviously, the more unknowns there are, the more cautious the approach which has to be adopted, but even where there is more than one unknown, analysis can nevertheless be a very useful valuation tool.

Many analyses will be much more involved than these examples, which are simply intended as a basic introduction to the process. If the valuer is careful to determine as many known facts as possible prior to embarking on analysis, and if he is then very methodical in his approach, there should be few problems encountered in doing more complicated analyses.

It should also be remembered that the results of analysis are likely to be more useful and more reliable the greater is the number of similar properties which can be analysed. Unfortunately, in the real world actual market evidence is often most evident for its absence, but nevertheless the valuer must attempt to use what evidence he has as intelligently as is possible.

CHAPTER 16

THE VALUATION OF VARYING INCOMES

It is possible for the income produced by a property to vary at different future dates. This may occur when a lease has been in existence for a number of years, during which time rental values have increased, the present rent consequently being out-of-date. When the current lease expires it is reasonable to assume that at least the present full rental value of the property would be obtainable on re-letting, and that this would produce a higher income-flow than the lower rent paid under the existing lease.

It is suggested that the present full rental value would be obtainable at the future date, as generally capital values are calculated by use of values which are known at the date of valuation. Any possibility of further increases in rental value between the present and the future is reflected conventionally by the choice of a lower yield for the valuation of a property, signifying that the risk entailed in investing is reduced by the prospect of an enhanced future rental value. Most values change with time because of inflation, and it is often suggested that valuers should attempt to calculate what future rental values will be by considering trends in value, and that valuations should then be made utilising anticipated future rents. This is not normally done, although in recent years changes in value have sometimes been substantial over relatively short periods of time to the extent that the valuer would be unwise to base his valuation only on past evidence. In such circumstances the valuer could consider what recent trends have been, whether they are likely to continue in the future, and whether values are likely to rise or fall, and if so at what rate and for how long. It is impossible to make accurate predictions of such matters, but the valuer has to remember that a current market valuation represents an estimate of the present value of all the future returns that will be produced by a property. Past transactions are historic evidence; the future could be very different and the valuer must therefore guard against placing unquestioning dependence upon comparables which are firmly based in the past.

Where an approach is utilised by the experienced valuer which entails building into a valuation a monetary allowance for future growth in rental value, the valuer should be careful not to adopt a low yield which also reflects the prospect of future rental growth, as if that were done growth prospects would be valued twice.

Nowadays, in certain valuation situations the valuer will be unable to base his valuation on the conventional approach which only allows for future rental growth through the choice of yield. Certain clients now demand valuations which include the estimation of future rental values and yields. In particular developers, who wish to know what possible developments will be worth when they are in due course completed, and financial institutions which lend money to finance development schemes, find valuations based on current market evidence of limited use to them. Their decisions are completely dependent upon estimates of values in the future and many of them demand valuations which actually incorporate predicted future rental values and market yields. However, currently the adoption of such a valuation approach is still the exception and most valuations are still done placing considerable reliance upon comparable evidence and current market rents and yields.

Varying rental incomes may also occur because of arrangements between the parties to a lease which have been made for their own convenience. A tenant may take a lease of a property in which he wishes to set up a business. The freeholder may agree to his occupation of the property for a number of years at a concessionary rent so that he may have a better chance of establishing his business. This may be in the interest of both parties, as it gives the businessman a greater chance of success, whilst the landlord will benefit from having a prosperous tenant. After the concessionary rental period, the businessman would normally pay the full market rental for the property.

Because of the rapid changes in value which occur during periods of high inflation, landlords are reluctant to enter into long leases at a fixed rent, as this might result in their receiving an income rapidly devalued by inflation. A series of short leases with new rents which kept pace with inflation would be preferable, but might not suit a potential tenant who would prefer the security of knowing that he had the right to occupy the premises concerned for a reasonable number of years. To satisfy the landlord's desire for a rent which does not rapidly become out-of-date, and the tenant's desire for security of possession of a property, leases are often arranged for a reasonably long term, with rent increases agreed for specific future dates. Also common are leases without pre-determined rental increases but with "rent-review" dates fixed in advance, with agreement on a specified way of assessing the rents to be fixed under these future reviews.

In order to consider the problems involved in valuing varying incomes, the principles will be discussed by reference to a freehold property which is let for a period of fifteen years. The rent for the next 5 years will be £10,000 per annum net, for the second 5 years it will be £15,000 per annum net, and for the final 5 years £20,000 per annum net.

The conventional valuation approach to the problem posed by a varying income-flow is to value each block of income separately and to add together the separate capital figures so found, the total being the present capital value of the right to receive all the items of future income. In effect, the valuer is faced with a series of separate valuations, as illustrated below.

First 5 years	Rent reserved £10,000 pa	
	× Multiplier	
	Capital value of first 5 years income-flow	£
Following 5 years	Rent reserved £15,000 pa	
	× Multiplier	
	Capital value of second 5 years income-flow	£
Final 5 years	Rent reserved £20,000 pa	
	× Multiplier	
	Capital value of final 5 years income-flow	£
Thereafter	Rent obtainable on re-letting	
	× Multiplier	£
	Present capital value of freehold interest = the sum of the present capital values of all the future income-flows	£

This format is used to value most varying incomes, and it is apparent that the answer will be influenced by the multipliers chosen. On page 97 it was shown that the Years' Purchase for a given number of years is in fact the sum of the Present Value of £1 figures for each of those years, and that the YP figures for specific periods at given rates of interest have for ease and convenience been provided in Parry's Tables. Using these tables, the capital value of the income-flow for the first five years can be found as follows:

First 5 years	Rent reserved	£10,000 pa
	YP for 5 years at 10%	3·7908
	Capital value of first 5 years income	£37,908

The only problem with this stage of the valuation is the choice of an appropriate rate of interest, which the valuer would select, using his market experience so that the risk of the investment was adequately reflected.

The income-flow for the second period can be tackled similarly and converted to a present capital sum.

Second 5 years	Rent reserved	£15,000 pa
	YP for 5 years at 10%	3·7908
	Capital value of the right to receive £15,000 per annum for the next 5 years	£56,862

The approach used is exactly the same as for the first years, but a problem has arisen. A YP for five years is the equivalent of adding the present values of £1 for each of the next five years to obtain a multiplier. When applied to the annual income of £15,000 this presupposes that £15,000 will be received this year, the second £15,000 in the second year, and so on for 5 years. But the first five years income-flow is £10,000 per annum and has already been valued, and the flow of £15,000 per annum will not commence until five years has elapsed. The position is therefore exactly the same as if a capital figure of £56,862 were not receivable until 5 years had elapsed. To find the value of the right to receive a future capital sum, the Present Value of £1 table can be used, as on page 89. The second stage of the valuation of the varying income then becomes

Second 5 years	Rent reserved	£15,000 pa
	YP for 5 years at 10%	3·7908
	Present capital value of the right to receive an income-flow of £15,000 per annum for 5 years, commencing this year	£56,862
	× PV of £1 in 5 years at 10%	0·6209213
	Present capital value of the right to receive an income flow of £15,000 per annum for 5 years which commences after the elapse of 5 years	£35,306·826

The valuation of the third income-flow involves exactly the same principles as those used for the second stage.

Third 5 years	Rent reserved	£20,000 pa
	YP for 5 years at 10%	3·7908

Capital value of income-flow of £20,000 per annum for 5 years	£75,816	
× PV of £1 in 10 years at 10%	0·3855433	
Present capital value of the right to receive an income-flow of £20,000 per annum for 5 years which commences after the elapse of ten years	£29,230·35	

In this third stage of the valuation a PV for 10 years has been used as that is the period which will elapse before the first year of the income-flow of £20,000 per annum is reached.

A problem arises on considering what would happen after the fifteenth year. The freehold interest should continue to provide an income-flow after the end of that year because the interest continues in perpetuity, and the property can therefore be re-let to produce another income-flow. The problem is, what rent can be expected from the property at that time? The value of the property is not confined to the first fifteen years, and an effort must be made to assess the value attributable to the period thereafter, that is from the fifteenth year in perpetuity.

Earlier in the chapter it was pointed out that it is conventional to value by reference to known current values, and it is therefore normally assumed that after the current lease has terminated it would be possible to re-let the property for the current full rental value. If on investigation it were found that the present full rental value of the property in the example was £25,000 per annum, the final stage of the valuation would become

Reversion after 15 years to Full Rental Value	£25,000	
YP in perpetuity at 10%	10	
Capital value of an income-flow of £25,000 per annum received in perpetuity	£250,000	
× PV of £1 in 15 years at 10%	0·2393920	
Present capital value of the right to receive £25,000 per annum in perpetuity commencing after the elapse of 15 years	£59,848	

The above calculation involves the use of two multipliers—10 and 0·2393920. The same result would emerge if these were multiplied together and the product applied to the annual income flow.

Reversion to Full Rental Value   £25,000 pa
    YP in perpetuity @ 10% =   10
    × PV of £1 in 15 years @ 10% = ·2393920   2·393920
                                    _____
                          Capital value   £59,848
                                                   _____

The figure 2·393920 is referred to as the Years' Purchase of a Reversion to a Perpetuity deferred 15 years at 10%. A YP of a Reversion to a Perpetuity can be calculated for given periods of deferment at given rates of interest. A table containing such calculations commences on page 41 of Parry's Tables and the figure 2·393920 can be looked up direct on page 52, so avoiding the need to refer to two separate tables.

Two multipliers were also used in each of the second and third stages of this valuation, and it is customary to apply the two multipliers to each other and then to utilise the product in the valuation, by which process the second stage would become:

                      Rent reserved   £15,000 pa
              YP for 5 years @ 10% 3·7908
        × PV of £1 in 5 years @ 10% 0·6209213   2·3537884
                                                _____
                                                £35,306·826
                                                _____

The valuation of each stage of varying income can be seen to involve the following basic process.

                                              Income-flow
        YP for period of income   ⎫
        × PV for period of deferment⎰   Multiplier
                                              _____
                                              Capital value
                                              _____

An easy way of understanding how long a period of deferment must be is to think of it as the period of waiting before the year in which an income-flow will commence.

Before reviewing the entire valuation there is a further modification which can be made to the different stages in order to comply with convention. In working through the different stages it was decided that the current full rental value of the property is £25,000 per annum net. The majority of valuers maintain that if at any time a property is occupied at less than its full rental value, that element of income is more secure than the receipt of the full rent would be. There is less risk of a lessee defaulting in the payment of rent if he is obtaining a property cheaply, as apart from the fact that a low rent is in any case easier to pay than the full rent, the tenant is hardly likely to run the risk of losing the profit which he is enjoying. Should he move elsewhere he would have to pay a higher rent for a similar property, so he is unlikely to do that. Should he not wish to use the property himself, if his lease allows him to sub-let, he could do so at the full market rent and make a profit. Consequently, whenever a rent paid is below the full market rental, it is generally considered to offer greater security to an investor. It is therefore valued at lower rates of interest, as it is reasoned that an investor would be prepared to accept a lower yield. The author considers that this theory is not always completely valid, but it is the conventional approach, and the valuation will now be reviewed, using progressively lower rates of interest as the rent reserved is lower.

Valuation

First 5 years		Rent reserved	£10,000 pa	
	YP for 5 years @ 8½%	3·9406		
				£39,406
Second 5 years		Rent reserved	£15,000 pa	
YP for 5 years @ 9%	3·8897			
× PV £1 in 5 years @ 9%	0·6499314			
		2·5280381		
			£37,920·571	
			£77,326·571	
Third 5 years		Rent reserved	£20,000 pa	
YP for 5 years @ 9½%	3·8397			
× PV £1 in 10 years @ 9½%	0·4035142			
		1·5493734		
			£30,987·468	
Reversion to Perpetuity		Full Rental Value	£25,000 pa	
YP in perpetuity @ 10% deferred 15 yrs	2·39392			
			59,848	
Capital value of freehold interest			£168,162·039	

A few further comments on this final valuation are necessary. It will be noted that where lower rates of interest have been used in the valuation a higher capital value results than when 10% was used to value the same stage. The greater security results in a higher capital value.

Some of the calculations have been made to as many as seven places of decimals. A valuer in practice would rarely do this, for a variety of reasons. Prior to the advent of cheap electronic calculators, such calculations were time-consuming and there-fore costly. As valuation cannot possibly be a precise science, it can also be argued that they are unnecessary. For the same reason it is also customary to round-off valuation answers to the type of figure which would be paid in the market, and the answer above would probably be "rounded-off" to either £167,500 or £168,000. Now that efficient calculators are available the author's preference is to do all calculations to about four places of decimals, confining "rounding-off" to the answer. Where a series of figures are all "rounded off" there is always the possibility of cumulative errors being unacceptably large. This will not often be the case and the degree of accuracy to which mathematics is done is very much a matter of personal choice to each valuer, although all approximations must be kept within acceptable limits.

The Years' Purchases for limited periods of time can be derived from the formulae

$$YP = \frac{1-V}{i} \text{ and } YP = \frac{1}{i + ASF}$$

The mathematical proofs of these formulae can be studied in "Modern Methods of Valuation", but a comparison with each of them and a YP from Parry's Tables will be made.

(i) YP for 10 years @ 8% = 6·7101
   (Parry's Tables, Page 34)

(ii) $YP = \dfrac{1-V}{i}$

V = PV of £1 in 10 years @ 8% = 0·4631935

$$i = \frac{8}{100} = 0·08$$

$$YP = \frac{1 - 0·4631935}{0·08} = \frac{0·5368065}{0·08} = 6·7101$$

(iii) $YP = \dfrac{1}{i + ASF}$

ASF 10 Years @ 8% = 0·0690295

$$YP = \frac{1}{0·08 + 0·0690295} = \frac{1}{0·1490295} = 6·7101$$

The above calculations have been done partly to show the reader that the formulae are in fact alternative and more rapid ways of working out YPs for limited periods, as opposed to adding together the PVs of £1 for the relevant time, and also to show that each of these three methods of finding the Y.P. is equally accurate.

... ...

CHAPTER 17

THE VALUATION OF
TERMINABLE INCOMES

Income-flows do not always continue in perpetuity and any income may be receivable for a limited number of years only, after which no income whatsoever is received. Such a situation arises when a leasehold interest in property is owned. Any income which it produces will end with the termination of the lease.

Many leasehold properties are occupied by the leaseholders and do not produce an actual income-flow. If, however, the full rental value is greater than the rent the leaseholder actually pays under his lease he enjoys a *"profit rent"*, as annual profit could be made if the property were sub-let at the full market value. Even if he continues in occupation he personally benefits from the profit rent, and the benefit of occupation at a cheap rent could be sold to another would-be occupier.

Only if a leasehold property produces or is occupied at a profit rent, will it have a value that can be calculated. The basic calculation for the valuation of a leasehold interest is

	Full Rental Value
Less	Rent Paid under the lease
	Profit rent
×	Multiplier
	Capital Value

Profit rents may occur for a variety of reasons. They may arise if rental values have increased since a lease began, or if a rent agreed under a lease is below the full market rent at the date of agreement. The latter may happen if a lessee pays a capital sum (a premium) at the commencement of a lease, representing rent or partial rent paid in advance. A lessee who pays a premium will only do so if he receives a reduction in rent to compensate him. Leaseholders sometimes pay all the rent for the duration of their lease in advance, and they thereafter occupy the property at a "peppercorn rent", which amounts to paying no rent at all.

Whatever the reason for its existence, if a profit rent does arise on a leasehold interest, an annual income-flow will exist in the form of that profit rent, and this could be attractive to investors.

When a freehold property is owned, the owner of the interest can expect the receipt of an income-flow in perpetuity, as he will always own the interest from which it arises. He will therefore always have a capital asset, and if the income-flow and the yield do not vary, then the capital value will always remain the same. Even if he decides to sell his interest, he will recoup his capital from the sale proceeds, and so his assets will remain intact.

In reality it is unlikely that the value of any freehold interest will remain exactly the same over a long period. Because of inflation, many rental values increase over time, whilst if buildings deteriorate or a location becomes less popular, rental values may decrease. Likewise, the underlying conditions of the market change frequently, with resultant changes in yields. However, the proposition that a freeholder always retains his asset and that his capital remains intact is basically true, and contrasts with the position of a leaseholder.

In the case of a leasehold interest, the leaseholder has the right to use and occupy the property only during the term of the lease. Once it expires he has no common law right to retain the use of the property, which returns to the control of the freeholder. As the unexpired term of a lease gets progressively shorter with the passage of time, so will the value of the leasehold interest decrease, until at the end of the lease no value remains.

If two similar quality investment properties produce equal income-flows, one being a freehold interest and the other a leasehold interest, an investor would obviously find the freehold a more attractive proposition. He would be prepared to pay less for the leasehold, and a valuation problem arises in determining what the difference in the value of two such properties should be.

Not only does the income-flow from a leasehold investment cease when the lease expires, but there are also other disadvantages. A freeholder, within the limits of common law and statutory law, can do what he likes with his property and is virtually "king of his castle". A leaseholder does not have unlimited freedom in the use of his property, being restricted by the terms of his lease. He may find that even if he has assigned or sub-let his property on the understanding that the new occupier will be responsible for complying with all the convenants and conditions of the lease, the freeholder may still be able to take action against him if the assignee or sub-lessee defaults. As the unexpired term of a lease grows shorter, it may prove very difficult to assign or sub-let a property, as most would-be occupiers require a reasonably long period of undisturbed occupation. What is often referred to as the "fag-end" of a lease may therefore be virtually unsaleable, and a leaseholder may be left with a property which neither he nor anybody else wishes to occupy for such a short period, but for which he nevertheless has to pay a rent.

The fact that a leaseholder has to pay rent at regular intervals, although not a particularly onerous task, involves management work, which does not arise with a freehold interest. A serious disadvantage with a leasehold property is that its value will eventually decrease even in inflationary times, and this lack of security in real terms is a most unattractive feature to investors. For these and other reasons a leasehold interest is generally considered less attractive than a freehold interest in a similar property, and investors therefore require higher yields from leasehold investments. The differences between freehold and leasehold yields may be as low as $\frac{1}{2}$% on good properties which are held on long leases and let to good tenants, increasing to 2% or more as the quality of the property becomes poorer and as the lease-term decreases.

The extra yield is not, however, sufficient to compensate a leaseholder for the eventual disappearance of his asset. If one investor spends £200,000 on a freehold investment, and another spends £200,000 on a leasehold investment, the latter will eventually lose his £200,000, whereas the freehold investor will always own the property on which he has spent his money. To ensure that he will not end up worse off financially through buying a leasehold interest, a wise leaseholder can set aside part of the annual income which his property produces, and can invest it to ensure that, by the time the leasehold interest terminates, his accumulated savings are sufficient to enable him to purchase another property which will produce a similar income-flow. If this is done the leaseholder will be no worse off in the long run that if he had purchased a freehold interest.

The fund which the leaseholder could establish is called an Annual Sinking Fund, because payments are made into it and compound interest is earned by it on an annual basis, and because it grows in size as the leasehold interest "sinks" in value.

The objective of a sinking fund is to recoup the capital invested in a wasting asset and in theory this can only be ensured if there is a guarantee that the money will be replaced by a specific date. Sinking fund theory is therefore based on the assumption that the annual instalments are placed in investments which are virtually risk-free. It is possible for a sinking fund policy to be taken out with an insurance company who will guarantee to pay a specified sum to the saver on a definite future date, in return for a series of annual premiums paid over the life of the policy. Because the insurance company guarantees payment of the future sum, the rate at which it pays interest on the annual instalments is low. The low rate reflects the low risk nature of the investment to the saver, and also leaves the insurance company a margin which it can earn on re-investment of the premiums. This will cover its overheads, and allow a profit to be made as payment for its expertise and its risk-taking. The insurance company will also discharge any tax liability and will pay interest on the sinking fund policy net of tax. For these reasons the interest earned on sinking fund policies ranges between about 2%–4% net of tax. These rates are not quite as low as they seem as if income tax is payable at for instance 40%, 2%–4% net of tax rates are in fact 3.34%–6.67% gross of tax.

The leasehold investor faces a slightly modified calculation when valuing his interest, as follows:

$$
\begin{array}{ll}
& \text{Net profit rent from property} \\
\textit{Less} & \textit{Annual Sinking Fund contribution} \\
\hline
& \text{Net spendable income} \\
\times & \text{YP} \\
\hline
& \underline{\text{Capital Value of Leasehold Interest}}
\end{array}
$$

The logic of this is not difficult to understand, but the mathematics provides a problem, as until the capital value is known, it is impossible to calculate the size of the required annual sinking fund instalment. The way in which the problem is overcome is by use of a modified Years' Purchase. When valuing a perpetual income a YP is found by use of the formula $\frac{1}{i}$. The 1 represents £1 of capital and i represents the annual earnings of that £1. The YP which results is the multiple that capital is of annual income. The multiplier theory is exactly the same with a terminable income, capital value being related to annual income. However, as part of the annual income of a leasehold property should be devoted to a sinking fund, the YP formula is modified to include a sinking fund allowance, becoming $\text{YP} = \frac{1}{i + . \text{SF}}$. The YP which results shows the multiple that capital value is of annual income after it has been separated into the annual spendable income and the sinking fund instalment.

The formula works in the following way, as illustrated by reference to an annual income of £10,000 arising from a leasehold interest which expires in 20 years' time. The potential investor can take out a sinking fund policy at $2\frac{1}{2}$% and requires a 10%

yield, and he wishes to know how much to pay for the investment.

The YP formula is $\dfrac{1}{i + SF}$

The annual sinking fund required to replace £1 of capital over 20 years at $2\frac{1}{2}\%$ is $0{\cdot}0391471$, and i is $0{\cdot}1$

$$YP = \frac{1}{i + SF} = \frac{1}{{\cdot}1 + {\cdot}0391471} = \frac{1}{{\cdot}1391471} = 7{\cdot}1866391$$

This can be found on page 4 of Parry's Tables as $7{\cdot}1866$.

The YP is then used in the normal way and applied directly to the total net income flow.

	Net Income	£10,000 pa
YP for 20 years @ 10% and $2\frac{1}{2}\%$		$7{\cdot}1866391$
	Capital Value	£71,866·391

The YP is stated to be at 10% and $2\frac{1}{2}\%$ and this is known as a *Dual Rate YP* as two different rates of interest are used in the calculation. The rate of 10% depicts the yield the investor requires or the rate at which he wishes to be remunerated by his investment, and it is referred to as the *"remunerative rate of interest"*. The rate of $2\frac{1}{2}\%$ shows the earning power of the sinking fund or the rate at which interest accumulates. It is referred to as the *"accumulative rate of interest"*.

An analysis of the above valuation will reveal the effectiveness of the YP.

Annual Income	£10,000
Yield required on capital invested	
$\dfrac{71866{\cdot}391 \times 10}{100}$ $=$	$7186{\cdot}6391$
Balance available for annual sinking fund	£2813·361
Annual Sinking Fund necessary to redeem £1 in 20 years @ $2\frac{1}{2}\%$ (Parry's Tables, page 80)	$0{\cdot}0391471$

Capital to be redeemed   £71,866·391

Annual Sinking Fund required to
accumulate to £71,866·391 over 20 years
at 2½%   £2813·3607

These calculations show that the YP has capitalised the income-flow in a manner which enables the correct yield to be obtained from the capital invested, and which also enables a sinking fund to be established out of income to recoup the original capital invested by the end of the lease. A final check proves that the sinking fund can achieve its objective.

Annual Sinking Fund   £2813·3607
Amount of £1 p.a. in 20 years @ 2½%   25·5447
Capital recouped after 20 years   £71,866·455

The figures in these calculations can be related to the layout shown on page 128

Net Income   £10,000 pa
Less Annual Sinking Fund   2813·3687

Spendable Income   £7186·6393
× YP in perpetuity @ 10%   10

Capital Value   £71,866·393

This illustrates the fact that once an allowance has been made out of income to keep the original capital intact, the remaining income can be treated as if it is receivable in perpetuity. This is logical, as at the end of the lease term the sinking fund of £71,866 can be used to purchase another investment which produces a 10% yield in perpetuity, or £7186·6 per annum.

Sinking Fund theory as applied to the valuation of terminable incomes is often criticised on the ground that it is unrealistic, and that no one would invest money to earn interest at only about 2½%. The fact that some investors do take out sinking fund policies with insurance companies rebuts this point. It is also often said that those who do so are unwise, as higher rates of interest could be earned, but if it is a basic requirement of an investor that the receipt of the future sum should be guaranteed, the requirement will not be achieved if acceptance of a higher yield reduces the security of capital. The choice between higher yields and absolute security must be the decision of individual investors, but whatever the criticisms of sinking fund theory may be, the resultant YP does ensure that an investor's original capital can be kept intact, and that he may be no worse off purchasing a leasehold investment than purchasing a freehold investment.

Another criticism of sinking fund theory is that in inflationary times it is unwise to base a decision on the recoupment of historic costs, and that provision should be made for the recoupment of a larger sum to allow for the ravages of inflation. If calculations were made on this basis, an investor would be allowing for part of the risk of his investment in the sinking fund. If by creating a larger sinking fund he eliminated the risk to his capital caused by inflationary trends, he would presumably be prepared to accept a lower remunerative rate of interest, as some of the risk normally reflected in this rate would have been removed. The use of a lower yield would then tend to cancel out the effects of creating a larger sinking fund. Instead of using the conventional dual rate YP approach valuations could quite easily be done using these other approaches and a discounted cash flow format as described in a later chapter.

Individual investors may obviously choose different ways of dealing with the sinking fund problem. Some may actually take out sinking fund policies with insurance companies at low rates of interest. Others may decide that rates offered by insurance companies are too low and that they will therefore put their sinking fund allowances into investments which, although not so risk-free, pay a higher rate of interest. Such a course of action may be quite acceptable, particularly if the period over which a sinking fund must accumulate is reasonably short or if the individual investor is sufficiently well-off to be able to carry some of the risk himself. Clearly, if an investor earns money on his sinking fund at a higher rate of interest than conventional theory suggests is appropriate, his annual sinking fund allowance need not be so large (that is if he merely wishes to recoup the historic cost of his investment). He can then bid more for a particular leasehold investment and still obtain the yield he desires. Whether in such circumstances he actually will bid more will depend on whether competition in the market forces him into a position of doing so, but clearly his advantageous sinking fund position would enable him to take such action if he so desired.

Investors with considerable property holdings may decide not to take out sinking fund policies, working on the principle that they can reinvest earnings themselves in other property purchases to earn a far higher rate of interest. This would be the likely attitude of a property investment company or a large institution. They could even organise their purchases such that a purchase of a wasting leasehold interest was balanced by a purchase of another asset which would appreciate over the same time period, the loss on one asset being compensated by the gain on the other.

In practice it is probably only a minority of purchasers of leasehold interests who actually take out sinking fund policies with insurance companies. Attitudes will vary depending upon the circumstances and outlooks of the individual investors, but those who reinvest what would be regarded as the sinking fund element in high yielding investments must appreciate that if they use this higher accumulative rate of interest in the valuation process they will, all other things being equal, increase their bid for a leasehold property. Such an action would narrow the gap in market values between the leasehold interest and freehold interests, and individual investors would have to make their own subjective decisions as to just how small they are prepared to see the differential become.

Valuation is in any event an imprecise science because of the very wide range of variables involved. It can be argued that the results obtained by valuing using conventional sinking fund theory are equally as acceptable as those to be obtained by using any of the alternatives. It might be argued that the use of a particularly low accumulative rate of interest in the valuation process would result in an unreasonably large sinking fund allowance. If that large sinking fund was in fact invested at a higher accumulative rate, then a sum larger than the historic cost of the asset would be recouped. Such a result, although occuring by a somewhat unsophisticated process, would in fact go some way towards answering the critics who suggest it is wrong only to allow for the recoupment of historic purchase costs.

Obviously a valuer should attempt to be as accurate as possible in all his calculations, and it is possible to dispense with the conventional approach and to allow for the recoupment of a future capital sum which attempts to allow for the change in values over the ownership of an asset. It is also possible to allow for this recoupment of capital using a higher accumulative rate of interest. As long as the valuer is aware of exactly what he is doing and of the problems in predicting the eventual capital sum required and the correct long term accumulative rate of interest, such a course of action is acceptable.

As a defence for conventional sinking fund theory, it is a fact that its use in the calculation of Dual Rate YPs results in the YPs for the valuation of terminable incomes being reduced substantially to reflect the unattractiveness of such incomes when compared with perpetual incomes.

The following examples illustrate the traditional approach to the valuation of varying incomes.

Example 1

A shop is held on a 21 year lease of which 14 years are unexpired. The full rental value is £20,000 per annum on full repairing and insuring terms, and the rent payable under the lease is £16,000 per annum on the same terms. The freehold interest in the property is considered to be an 8% risk.

	Full Rental Value	£20,000 pa
Less	Rent paid under lease	£16,000 pa
	Profit rent	£ 4,000 pa
	YP for 14 years @ 9%/2½%	6·6429
	Capital Value of Leasehold Interest	£26,571·60

Note. If there was no profit rent, the capital value would be nil.

The leasehold rate of 9% is 1% above the freehold rate, to reflect the disadvantages of leasehold interests. The sinking fund is calculated at 2½%.

"Full repairing and insuring terms" refers to the agreement in the lease regarding repairing and insuring liabilities. When a property is let on *F.R.I.* terms, as they are abbreviated, the lessee is responsible for all repairs and for insuring the property.

If the lessee could sub-let his property on the same terms, he could pass on the liability for these items to the sub-lessee, so no deduction is necessary in the valuation, as he would not have to pay for these items on sub-letting.

Example 2

A shop is occupied on a lease with 12 years unexpired at a rent of £6,000 per annum for the next 5 years and £7,000 per annum thereafter. It is held on F.R.I. terms and the full rental value on the same terms is £9,000. The freehold risk rate is 7%.

Next 5 years		F.R.V.	£9,000 pa	
	Less	Rent paid under lease	£6,000 pa	
		Profit Rent	£3,000 pa	
		YP 5 years @ 8%/2½%	3·7003	
				£11,100
Last 7 years		F.R.V.	£9,000 pa	
	Less	Rent paid under lease	£7,000 pa	
		Profit Rent	£2,000 pa	
		YP 7 years @ 8%/2½% 4·7060		
		× PV £1 in 5 years @ 8% 0·6805832	3·2028	£ 6,406
		Capital Value of Leasehold Interest		£17,506

SAY £17,500

Note. The method used to defer the income which is not received until 5 years have elapsed is the same as that used in Chapter Sixteen.

There is no variation in the rate of interest used for the two periods, as it is assumed that in both periods the property could and would be sub-let at the full rental value. The receipt of rent would therefore always be at full risk.

Single Rate Years' Purchase

In Chapter Sixteen the same formula as that used in this chapter was used to find the Years' Purchase appropriate for the valuation of varying incomes. In that chapter, however, it was used to calculate what is known as the Single Rate Years' Purchase, which is a YP calculated using the same rate of interest for the remunerative rate and for sinking fund calculations. A comparison between Single Rate and Dual Rate YP's is shown below.

Single Rate YP for 10 years @10%

$$YP = \frac{1}{i + SF}$$

$i = ·1$
ASF to redeem £1 in 10 years
@ 10% = ·0627454

$$YP = \frac{1}{·1 + ·0627454}$$

$$YP = \frac{1}{·1627454}$$

$$YP = 6·1445669$$

Dual Rate YP for 10 years @ 10% and 2½%

$$YP = \frac{1}{i + SF}$$

$i = ·1$
ASF to redeem £1 in 10 years
@ 2½% = ·0892588

$$YP = \frac{1}{·1 + ·0892588}$$

$$YP = \frac{1}{·1892588}$$

$$YP = 5·2837701$$

It can be seen that the only difference in the calculations results from the use of different rates for the sinking funds. The YP's are, however, used in different circumstances, and the Single Rate YP is used in the valuation of incomes produced by freehold interests, when the rôle of the sinking fund in the formula is to make an arithmetical adjustment to the YP merely to permit valuations to be made for a limited period. In freehold valuations there is no suggestion that a sinking fund should actually be established, as there is no need to recoup capital, none being lost with the passage of time. The ASF is a reducing agent in the formula to "devalue" the YP so that no value is attached to the period during which an income does not flow.

To illustrate that the single rate YP formula does effectively adjust YP's to allow for time differentials, an income of £10,000 per annum receivable in perpetuity will be valued at a 10% rate of interest.

Annual Income	£ 10,000
YP in perpetuity @ 10%	10
Capital Value	£100,000

This valuation could be done in two stages, and, unless the technique used is faulty, the valuation of an income of £10,000 per annum for 10 years followed by the valuation of a reversion to £10,000 per annum in perpetuity, should give the same total as the calculation above.

Next 10 years	Annual Income		£ 10,000
	YP for 10 years @ 10%		6·1446
			£ 61,446

Reversion	Annual Income	£10,000	
YP in perpetuity @ 10%	10		
× PV £1 in 10 years @ 10%	0·38554	3·8554	£ 38,554
		Capital Value	£100,000

The arithmetical adjustment in the YP formula effected by the sinking fund element of the denominator has allowed for the correct apportionment of the income over time.

The use of a *Dual Rate YP* envisages the need actually to establish a fund to accumulate money in circumstances in which it can only be invested to earn interest at a rate which differs from that earned by the property investment.

CHAPTER 18

TAXATION AND VALUATION

Taxation has only been mentioned in passing, but, as most people are only too well aware, it plays a very important and prominent rôle in modern life, to the extent that income is frequently very much reduced after tax liabilities have been met. Almost all income is assessable for tax purposes, although, depending upon personal circumstances and the detailed provisions of particular tax systems, taxpayers may get various allowances and expenses against their income to reduce their liability. In the United Kingdom, earnings from certain sources, such as National Savings Certificates, are not taxed, while certain earnings, such as interest earned on building society accounts, are paid net of tax. The general rule, however, is that most income is taxable, and because there is often a wide discrepancy between earnings gross of tax and the same earnings net of tax, the majority of people are more interested in knowing the size of the latter. The wage-earner looks at the last figure on his pay-slip to discover what is left for him to spend after the "taxman" has had "his share", and the majority of investors will also be principally interested in knowing what is left for them at the end of the day.

Because there is a wide variation in incomes, depending upon many factors such as the type of job or profession in which they are earned, whether they are earned in a high wage area or a low wage area, and the age of the earner, and because different earners have different allowances to set against tax, resulting from differing personal circumstances, there is a very wide range of average rates of liability to tax. Although the basic United Kingdom rate of income-tax is currently 27p in the £, probably very few people have that rate as the average rate of tax for their total income.

During the 1980's in the United Kingdom, there have been considerable reductions in income-tax rates. Prior to these reductions, there were periods when total tax on income was in some circumstances, as high as 98p in the £ on large incomes. There were also periods during which investment income was subject to a higher tax than other income, to the extent that although income from employment might have been subject to a maximum tax of 60p in the £, investment income was subject to an

additional investment income surcharge of 15% giving a total
liability of 75p in the £. Average liabilities may range from nil
if total allowances exceed total income, to a figure approaching
60p in the £ if an income is large.

Because of the very wide range of possible tax liabilities, yields
from investments are normally quoted gross of tax, as it would
be difficult to decide what adjustment would be appropriate to
the majority of investors if yields were to be quoted net of tax.
Also, if yields were quoted net of tax it would be difficult to
compare yields over extended periods of time, as any tax changes
would result in revisions of net of tax yields, making immediate
comparison impossible. Consequently, yields from stocks and
shares, loans and property are conventionally quoted as the yield
before income-tax has been deducted, and investors must allow
for their own personal tax liability if they wish to find out the
net-of-tax yield.

There is a school of thought which considers that valuers
should use net-of-tax incomes and yields in their calculations,
as, in a similar way to sinking fund allowances, tax liabilities
cannot be spent by an investor. To include them in calculations
amounts to valuing an element of income which the investor
does not in fact receive. This is a perfectly sound argument,
but the valuer should always give consideration to the purpose
of a valuation before he decides on appropriate tactics. When
a valuation is being made to find the market value of a property,
if all the potential purchasers are valuing on a gross-of-tax basis,
that must be the appropriate approach to use in order to determine the market value their competition would create. On the
other hand, the valuer would be perfectly justified in valuing
on a net basis if his instructions were to determine the value
of a property to a particular investor, in which case he could
allow for that individual's tax liability. The market value and
the value to the individual might in fact be quite different.

Perpetual Income and Net-of-Tax Valuations

When an income is receivable in perpetuity, a valuation will
give exactly the same answer whether calculations are done gross
or net-of-tax. To illustrate the fact, an income of £10,000 pa
annum receivable in perpetuity at a gross of tax yield of 10%
will be considered.

Valuation

Annual income	£	10,000
YP in perpetuity @ 10%		10
Capital value		£100,000

The same income will now be considered on a net basis from the point of view of a person paying tax at 40p in the £.

For every £1 of income he receives the tax payment will be 40p and his net-of-tax income will be 60p. Therefore, if he invests £100 at 10% gross, his gross-of-tax income will be £10, whilst his net-of-tax income will be £6, giving a net-of-tax yield of 6%. In valuing a net-of-tax income, the net-of-tax yield must obviously be used for consistency and accuracy, and the value to the taxpayer is found as follows:

Annual income	£ 10,000
Less Income tax @ 40p	4,000
Net-of-tax income	£ 6,000
YP in perpetuity at net-of-tax yield of 6%	16·666
Capital value	£100,000

If the investor had a tax liability of 80p in the £ the calculation would be:

Annual income	£ 10,000
Less Income tax at 80p	£ 8,000
Net-of-tax income,	£ 2,000
YP in perpetuity at net-of-tax yield of 2%	50
Capital value	£100,000

With an unvarying income receivable in perpetuity the gross-of-tax and net-of-tax approach will always give exactly the same answer, irrespective of differing tax liabilities.

Varying Incomes and Net-of-Tax Valuations

An income of £10,000 per annum receivable for 10 years with a reversion to a perpetual income of £20,000 per annum will be considered. For illustration purposes a gross of tax rate of 10% will be used throughout.

Gross-of-Tax Valuation

Annual income	£10,000
YP for 10 years @ 10%	6·1446
	£ 61,446

Reversion to income in perpetuity	£20,000	
YP in perpetuity @ 10% deferred 10 years	3·85543	
		£ 77,108·60
Capital value		£138,554·60

The same income will be considered on a net-of-tax basis with a tax liability of 40p in the £, in which case the net of tax yield is 6%.

Net-of-Tax @ 40p Valuation

Annual income	£10,000	
Less Tax @ 40p	£ 4,000	
Net-of-tax income	£ 6,000	
YP for 10 years @ 6%	7·3601	
		£ 44,160·6
Reversion to income in perpetuity	£20,000	
Less Tax @ 40p	£ 8,000	
Net-of-tax income	£12,000	
YP in perpetuity @ 6% deferred 10 years	9·30658	
		£111,678·96
Capital value		£155,839·56

This valuation gives a much higher result than the gross-of-tax valuation, and a valuation for an 80p tax liability will also differ.

Net-of-Tax @ 80p Valuation

Annual Income	£10,000	
Less Tax @ 80p	£ 8,000	
Net of tax income	£ 2,000	
YP for 10 years @ 2%	8·9826	
		£ 17,965·20
Reversion to income in perpetuity	£20,000	
Less Tax @ 80p	£16,000	
Net-of-tax income	£ 4,000	
YP in perpetuity @ 2% deferred 10 years	41·01741	
		£164,069·64
Capital value		£182,034·84

Yet again a higher value results than that found by use of the gross-of-tax method. There is nothing magical about these differences. They arise purely as a result of discounting the future at different rates of interest, and if reference is made to page 89 it will be recalled that the lower the rate of interest that is used, the higher the future is valued in comparison to the present. Consequently, if there is an increase in income at a future date, the lower the rate of interest used, the higher will be the value placed on the future rental increase, and the lower the relative value placed on the immediate income.

In terms of YP's this fact can be illustrated as follows by reference to the three valuations.

	Gross Basis (10%)	Net of Tax @ 40p(6%)	Net of Tax @ 80p(2%)
YP for first 10 years	6·1446	7·3601	8·9826
YP for reversion	3·85543	9·30658	41·01741
Total YP's used	10·00003	16·66668	50·00001
% of YP's allocated to first 10 years	61·45%	44·16%	18%
% of YPs allocated to reversion	38·55%	55·84%	82%

The last two lines show quite clearly the change in the apportionment of values between the term and reversion as the rate of interest decreases. As the use of a net rate of interest inevitably involves a reduction in the rate, net-of-tax valuations will throw up this pattern of values whenever there is a future increase in rent.

Although the Gross-of-Tax and Net-of-Tax approaches can lead to considerable differences in the results obtained in a valuation, the student should remember that in the market most valuations are in fact done on a gross-of-tax basis. if the market values in this way, then the gross-of-tax approach must be used to find market value, but the significance of the net-of-tax approach to the individual investor must always be remembered.

Tax and the Valuation of Leasehold Properties

Liability to income-tax creates a problem in the valuation of leasehold interests that does not exist with freehold interests. A major difference between the two types of valuation is that in leasehold valuations the rental income is allocated partly to an annual sinking fund to recoup the capital invested, the remainder being spendable income.

In order to examine the problem caused by the burden of income-tax, a leasehold property which produces a profit rent of £1,000 per annum for the next 12 years will be considered. A yield of 10% is required and a sinking fund can be established to accumulate at 3%.

Valuation

Profit rent	£1,000 pa
YP for 12 years @ 10% and 3%	5·8664
Capital value	£5,866·4

A yield of 10% on £5,866·4 is £586·64 per annum. The ASF contribution is therefore £1,000 – £586·64 or £413·36

(or ASF to recoup £1 in 12 years @ 3%
$$= 0·0704621 \times \text{Capital } £5,866·4 = £413·36)$$

If the owner of the leasehold interest has to pay income-tax at 40p in the £ the following overall pattern results.

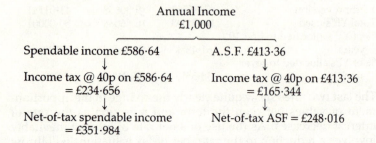

Annual Income
£1,000

Spendable income £586·64	A.S.F. £413·36
↓	↓
Income tax @ 40p on £586·64 = £234·656	Income tax @ 40p on £413·36 = £165·344
↓	↓
Net-of-tax spendable income = £351·984	Net-of-tax ASF = £248·016

The total tax payment is £234·656 + £165·344, which is £400 or 40p in £ on £1,000.

It is quite apparent that if an ASF contribution of £413·36 is necessary to recoup the capital of £5,866·4 over 12 years, annual contributions which have been reduced by tax to £248·016 cannot possibly achieve the same objective. The ASF contributions must therefore be increased to the original £413·36, but if extra money is taken from the spendable income the correct yield will not be obtained from the investment.

The solution which is adopted is to increase the original ASF contributions so that after income tax has been paid on them they are still large enough to recoup the original capital. As the ASF contribution is increased, the spendable income must be reduced, but if the bid for the property interest is at the same time reduced so that the spendable income gives the correct yield on capital, the investor will achieve all his objectives.

The ASF contributions are increased in the ratio of income before tax to income after tax by multiplying the ASF by the equation $\dfrac{100}{100 - \text{Tax}}$. This process is done within the YP formula, which becomes

$$YP = \frac{1}{i + SF \times \dfrac{100}{100 - T}}$$

If this formula is used to obtain the YP for 12 years at 10% and 3% allowing for income-tax at 40p in the £, the calculation becomes:

$$YP = \frac{1}{\cdot 1 + (\text{ASF to recoup £1 in 12 years @ 3\%)} \times \dfrac{100}{100 - 40}}$$

$$= \frac{1}{\cdot 1 + (\cdot 0704621)(100/60)}$$

$$= \frac{1}{\cdot 1 + \cdot 1174368} = \frac{1}{\cdot 2174368} = 4 \cdot 5990375$$

This is known as the Years' Purchase for 12 years at 10% and 3% adjusted for tax at 40p in the £. The effect of the adjustment for tax has been to reduce the size of the YP from 5·8664, and to increase the ASF allowance for the recoupment of each £1 of capital invested from £0·0704621 to £0·1174368.

The interest will now be valued, using the new YP, and the result will then be analysed.

Profit Rent	£1,000
YP for 12 years @ 10% and 3% adjusted for tax at 40p in £	4·5990375
Capital value	£4,599·0375

Annual income
£1,000

Spendable income	Annual sinking fund
10% of £4,599·0375	£1,000 − £459·9
= £459·9	= £540·1
	↓
	Income tax @ 40p = £216·04
	↓
	Net-of-tax ASF = 540·1
	− 216·04 = £324·06

The ASF can be checked for effectiveness

ASF net of tax	£324·06
× Amount of £1 pa for 12 years @ 3%	14·1920
Capital recouped	£4,599·0595

It can be seen that the adjusted YP has reduced the purchase price sufficiently to enable both the correct yield to be obtained from the investment and the capital to be recouped, despite the tax burden on the sinking fund element of the income. If the tax liability at 40p on the spendable income is checked, it will be found to be £183·96, giving a net-of-tax spendable income of £275·94 and a total tax liability of £400.

A similar adjustment to the sinking fund can be made to allow for any rate of tax, and the valuation could be done to reflect the value to an investor paying tax at 60p in £.

Profit Rent   £   1,000

YP for 12 years @ 10% and 3% adjusted for tax at 60p

$$\frac{1}{i + (\cdot0704621) \dfrac{100}{100 - 60}} = \frac{1}{\cdot1 + (\cdot0704621) \dfrac{100}{40}}$$

$$= \frac{1}{\cdot1 + \cdot1761552} = \frac{1}{\cdot2761552} \qquad\qquad = 3\cdot6211521$$

Capital value   £3,621·1521

As income tax-liability increases, so does the value decrease, simply because a greater sinking fund allocation becomes necessary. This reduces the spendable income, and therefore the capital value to the taxpayer also falls.

Sinking Fund Earnings and Income-Tax

Earlier in the book it was mentioned that the interest rate earned on sinking fund policies was usually quoted on a net-of-tax basis, that is on the assumption that tax was paid by the insurance company prior to payment to the policy holder. The YP calculations above were made on this assumption and the Dual Rate YP figures in Parry's Tables are compiled on the same assumption. There is therefore no need to make any adjustment in the YP formula for this tax burden.

It should be remembered that the rate at which a sinking fund earns money is not quite as low as the net-of-tax rate of interest makes it appear. If income-tax is paid at 40p in £, 3% net-of-tax is the equivalent of 5% before tax, and in the examples above this would be the gross of tax rate of interest on the sinking fund.

To adjust rates of interest to allow for tax, gross rates can be reduced to a net-of-tax rate by using the formula:

$$\text{Gross rate} \times \frac{100 - T}{100} = \text{Net rate}$$

Net rates can be increased to a gross-of-tax rate by using the formula:

$$\text{Net rate} \times \frac{100}{100 - T} = \text{Gross rate}$$

In each case T represents the rate of tax quoted as a percentage or as pence in the £.

The Remunerative Rate of Interest and Income-Tax

In none of the calculations made above was any adjustment made to the remunerative rate of interest to allow for tax payments on the spendable income. This is because the convention is to quote all yields on a gross-of-tax basis for comparison purposes, and unless a valuer has a specific reason for departing from the conventional approach, no adjustment is made to the yield in respect of income-tax liability.

The Use of Tax-Adjusted Dual Rate Years' Purchase Tables

The valuer should use tax-adjusted tables whenever a valuation is made of a leasehold property for which the potential purchasers are tax-payers. If circumstances are unusual enough for all the would-be purchasers to be exempt income-tax, there is no need for tax-adjusted YP's. When tax-adjusted tables are used it is normal for them to be adjusted at the standard rate of income-tax. For correct usage the rate of tax adopted should really be that which is likely to apply to the potential purchasers of the interest concerned, although this may not necessarily be easy to determine, or the rate applicable to the client for whom a valuation is being made.

CHAPTER 19

DISCOUNTED CASH FLOW TECHNIQUES

The use of discounted cash flow techniques is said by some to have been introduced into property valuation in the last decade or so, and in the relatively recent past one heard discussions as to whether this was a welcome development and whether such techniques were proper and acceptable methods of valuation. Although it would be inappropriate in an introductory text-book to go too deeply into this subject area, in view of the increasing prominence of this topic it is essential to consider it. There is no intention of providing anything other than a basic introduction to the topic, and the reader will be able to follow this up with further study in more advanced books.

It is appropriate to recall some of the fundamental points made previously in this book. Valuation is a method of assessing the various advantages and disadvantages of an interest in property and expressing them in money terms. When we place valuations on them we enable different properties with different advantages and disadvantages to be compared with each other in money terms. Discounted cash flow techniques facilitate such comparisons, and it is worth considering why they have become popular in recent years, and, conversely, why they were not used more widely previously. In posing these questions it must be stated that it is the author's opinion that such techniques have in fact been used by valuers for a very long time, although not in the same format as today. It is hoped the reasons for this opinion will shortly become apparent.

The traditional approach to the valuation of an income flow from a property has already been considered and is as below.

Example 1

What is the value of an income flow for the next four years of £10,000 per annum payable in arrears from a freehold property if the property is considered to be an 8% risk?

Net Income	£10,000 p.a.
YP for 4 years @ 8%	3·3121
Capital Value	£33,121

As considered in Chapter 14 the Present Value of £1 per annum (or the YP) is nothing more than an addition of the present values of £1 for each of the years under consideration, so the above calculation could have been achieved by the following alternative method.

Example 2
First year's income: £10,000 × PV £1 in 1 year @ 8%
$$= £10,000 × 0.9259259 \qquad = £9,259.259$$
Second year's income: £10,000 × PV £1 in 2 years @ 8%
$$= £10,000 × 0.8573388 \qquad = £ 8,573.388$$
Third year's income: £10,000 × PV £1 in 3 years @ 8%
$$= £10,000 × 0.7938322 \qquad = £ 7,938.322$$
Fourth year's income: £10,000 × PV £1 in 4 years @ 8%
$$= £10,000 × 0.7350299 \qquad = £ 7,350.299$$

	Total capital value	£33,121.268

The addition of the present values of £1 for each of the four years gives a figure of 3.3121, or the Present Value of £1 Per Annum for 4 years at 8% as used in Example 1.

What is made clear by the layout in Example 2 is that we have taken a series of cash flows and have discounted them to the present. The abbreviated layout of Example 1 does not make this so apparent, but from this we can see that the traditional methods of valuation are in fact techniques of discounting cash flows.

It is therefore not true to say that the use of discounted cash flow techniques is new in property valuation. What has happened in recent years is that more sophisticated and more complex discounted cash flow calculations have been done, and that more variables and different layouts have been utilised for valuations. The two are very much related to each other in that the building into a valuation of more variables entails more calculations, and a new format to take account of the more complex nature of the valuation is a logical development.

There are numerous reasons why these more complex valuations have been adopted in recent years, but in general they derive from two main factors: firstly, there is probably a need for more complex valuations and, secondly, the machinery to perform complex calculations is now cheaply available to all valuers, making such calculations a practical proposition. The need for more complex valuations arises because there are now many properties available for purchase which cost many millions of pounds. When such large sums of money are being committed for many years to come it is essential that the purchasers look very carefully at their commitments, taking into account in their valuations every conceivable variable which could affect the ultimate price at which they purchase, or, looked at from the vendor's viewpoint, at which the property sells. The need for care and precision in valuation is even greater if the vendors or purchasers are trustees of funds for others, as will often be the case with pension funds, insurance companies and other institutions which are active in the property market.

The need for complex valuations also arises from background factors which were perhaps not so important in past years. In the past it was often possible to borrow large sums of money for long periods at fixed rates of interest. Nowadays, it is likely that the cost of borrowing will be related to other variable factors, such as the base lending rates of banks, and there may therefore be a need to build into a valuation calculation variations to allow for anticipated changes in the cost of finance. Taxation is likewise more complex than in the past, and it may also be necessary to build in variables to allow for known or anticipated future changes in tax commitments. Similarly, if an important factor in the appraisal process is an element of tax relief on interest charges on borrowed funds, it may also be necessary to take account in the appraisal of variations in the amount of interest payable in the future and consequent variations in anticipated tax relief.

These, and other factors, give rise to the need for complex appraisal calculations which only a few years ago would have proved exceedingly difficult for all but a few large and well equipped firms. Not only that, but such calculations would have been too time consuming in most instances, as valuations are regularly required at short notice. The electronic calculator has changed that situation and, as long as he understands what he is attempting to do, any valuer can now perform involved and difficult calculations with speed and ease. The development of computing technology has assisted the development of investment valuation and analysis techniques.

There is now no excuse for avoiding complex valuation calculations. Equally, though, there is no point in using them unless there is a need for their use, and unless they provide as good, and preferably better, a result than the simpler, traditional approach would provide. If there is no positive benefit to be obtained from using the more elaborate approach, then there is no point in using it.

Whenever modern discounted cash flow techniques are used it is well worth remembering that they are nothing more than variations on the basic compound interest theme which is the basis of all valuations. All future receipts and liabilities are discounted to a common date to enable an accurate appraisal to be made and, quite frequently, to enable comparison to be made with other investments for which the same exercise has been carried out.

There are several kinds of discounted cash flow appraisal but consideration will be restricted to the two most commonly used, the Net Present Value method and the Internal Rate of Return method.

Net Present Value Method

This is just like the investment method of valuation in that all future items are discounted to a net present value by using compound interest calculations. However, whereas in an investment valuation it is conventional only to consider the net income of each year, the use of a tabular format for the Net Present Value method facilitates the inclusion as separate items in the appraisal of all items of income and expenditure for each year. The valuer can decide whether he will then in fact simply discount the net income or the net deficit for each year to the present, or whether, if there is sound reason for so doing, he will discount items of income and expenditure separately using different rates of interest for the purpose as appropriate. Not only can different rates of interest be utilised but calculations can be made for individual items at more precise dates rather than at the end of each year, which the conventional investment valuation presupposes.

The precise layout can be varied to suit the requirements of an appraisal or the preferences of a valuer, but a typical layout is illustrated below.

End of Year	Particulars	Outflow	Inflow	Net Flow + or −	PV of £1	Net Outflow	Net Inflow

The use of the method can best be illustrated by consideration of examples. In each case it will be assumed for simplicity that calculations are needed at twelve monthly intervals, although different time periods could be utilised as required.

Example 3

Property A is available at a purchase price of £100,000 and the total costs of purchase would be £8,000. It is let at a rent of £11,000 per annum receivable in arrears on full repairing and insuring terms for the next four years. The potential purchaser expects that he would sell the property after four years for £140,000, the total costs on the sale being £6,000.

End of Year	Particulars	Outflow	Inflow	Net Flow + or −	PV of £1 @12%	Net Outflow	Net Inflow
0	Purchase Price	100,000					
	Purchase Costs	8,000		−108,000	1	108,000	
1	Rent		11,000	+11,000	·8928571		9,821
2	Rent		11,000	+11,000	·7971939		8,769
3	Rent		11,000	+11,000	·7117802		7,830
4	Rent		11,000				
	Sale Proceeds		140,000				
	Sale Costs	6,000		+145,000	0·6355181		92,150
						108,000	118,570

Net Present Value +10,570

Note: Outgoings on management have been ignored in this example for simplicity.

A rate of 12% has been chosen (known as the "target rate") and at this rate the calculations show that in net present value terms the investment shows a positive balance of £10,570 representing an excess of inflows over outflows. A positive balance at the end of net present value calculations suggests that an investment will be worth entering into as it should be viable at the target rate. Conversely, if there is a deficit at the end of the calculations the inference is that it will prove an unacceptable investment. If net outflows and net inflows are exactly equal the investment will earn money at the same rate as that used in the calculation and will be an acceptable investment as it should not entail loss.

In choosing a rate of interest of 12% it may be that the investor is influenced by the fact that this is the cost of money to him: he has to pay 12% per annum interest on money he borrows. It may be that he has no need to borrow money, and 12% is the opportunity cost of his own money; he is prepared to invest if he can get that rate of return on the money he invests. Again, the choice of 12% may be made because he regards the property which produces the income as a 12% risk when compared with all the other investments in which he could place his money.

Whatever influences his choice of rate the above calculations show that his "target rate" of 12% is achieved with a bonus of £10,570. In effect the rate of return on the investment is in excess of 12% per annum. It should be noted that this will be the case as long as the predictions of inflows and outflows are correct, and as long as the appropriate rate remains at 12%.

It is worth considering what happens when the target rate is altered.

Example 4

The same facts as in Example 3, but a rate of 16% is used instead of 12%.

End of Year	Particulars	Outflow	Inflow	Net Flow + or −	PV of £1 @16%	Net Outflow	Net Inflow
0	Purchase Price	100,000					
	Purchase Costs	8,000		−108,000	1	108,000	
1	Rent		11,000	+11,000	·8620690		9,483
2	Rent		11,000	+11,000	·7431629		8,175
3	Rent		11,000	+11,000	·6406577		7,047
4	Rent		11,000				
	Sale Proceeds		140,000				
	Sale Costs	6,000		+145,000	0·5522911		80,082
						108,000	104,787

Net Present Value   −3,213

Note: Outgoings on management have been ignored in this example for simplicity.

The calculations show that if the target rate is 16% the investment will not be acceptable if the predictions of inflows and outflows are correct. The investment shows a deficit over the four years of £3,213 when all future costs and returns are translated into terms of present value.

What was an acceptable investment at a target rate of 12% is not so at 16%; somewhat between these two figures will be a rate of interest at which net outflows and net inflows are exactly equal, and this figure will be the rate of return on the investment. The investor must then decide whether this rate of return is acceptable.

The rate of discount is critical as it determines whether an investment will be regarded as acceptable or not. It can be seen that an investment may be attractive to a person who can borrow money at 12%, but unattractive to someone who has less favourable borrowing terms.

The Net Present value approach is a very useful method of analysis and enables investors to determine whether investments are likely to prove acceptable at a given target rate.

It also enables alternative investments to be compared to show which will give the biggest profit (or the biggest loss). There may be occasions on which expenditure cannot be avoided, and if a loss of some sort is inevitable it may be helpful to know which option will give rise to the smallest loss. Its use as a method of comparison will be considered in the following example and by subsequent comparison with Example 3.

Example 5

Another property, Property B, is on offer at £85,000 for which the expenses of purchase would be £4,000. It is let for four years on internal repairing terms at a rent of £10,500 per annum receivable in arrears. It is anticipated that it could be sold after four years for £112,000 the estimated costs of sale being £3,000.

End of Year	Particulars	Outflow	Inflow	Net Flow + or −	PV of £1 @12%	Net Outflow	Net Inflow
0	Purchase Price	85,000					
	Purchase Costs	4,000		−89,000	1	89,000	
1	Rent		10,500				
	Repairs	700					
	Insurance	220					
	Management	525		+9,055	·8928571		8,085
2	Rent		10,500				
	Repairs	770					
	Insurance	242					
	Management	525		+8,963	·7971939		7,145
3	Rent		10,500				
	Repairs	847					
	Insurance	266					
	Management	525		+8,862	·7117802		6,308
4	Rent		10,500				
	Repairs	932					
	Insurance	293					
	Management	525					
	Sale Proceeds		112,000				
	Sale Costs	3,000		+117,750	0·6355181		74,832
						89,000	96,370

Net Present Value   +7,370

Note: Management costs are calculated as 5% of rent received.

In this case there is a predicted profit in net present value terms of £7,370 using a target rate of 12%. At 12% Property A produced £10,570 above the target return which is 30·27% greater but on an initial investment which required 21·35% more capital. It therefore appears that Property A would be more attractive, although much may depend on whether there are problems in raising the extra £19,000 capital.

Whatever the circumstances, if our investor needs a steady income for each of the next four years Property B will not be attractive. The calculations have been made on the not unreasonable assumption that the costs of repair and insurance will rise by 10% per annum, and this would result in a decreasing annual income. This may make investment B less attractive to the investor especially if he requires an income flow to meet commitments which may increase with inflation. The arrangements he could make with the balance of £19,000 which would be saved on the purchase of Property B would be an important factor in determining the eventual investment decision, although it would appear unlikely that arrangements could be made which would tip the balance in favour of Property B.

A consideration of the effect a higher discount rate would have on Property B should be made to complete the picture.

Example 6
The same facts as in Example 5, but a target rate of 16% is used instead of 12%.

End of Year	Particulars	Outflow	Inflow	Net Flow + or −	PV of £1 @ 16%	Net Outflow	Net Inflow
0	Purchase Price	85,000					
	Purchase Costs	4,000		−89,000	1	89,000	
1	Rent		10,500				
	Repairs	700					
	Insurance	220					
	Management	525		+9,055	·8620690		7,806
2	Rent		10,500				
	Repairs	770					
	Insurance	242					
	Management	525		+8,963	·7431629		6,661
3	Rent		10,500				
	Repairs	847					
	Insurance	266					
	Management	525		+8,862	·6406577		5,678
4	Rent		10,500				
	Repairs	932					
	Insurance	293					
	Management	525					
	Sale Proceeds		112,000				
	Sale Costs	3,000		+117,750	·5522911		65,032
						89,000	85,177

Net Present Value −3,823

Note: Management costs are calculated as 5% of rent received.

The effect of the higher target rate is again to make the investment unacceptable. Whereas with Property A the deficit at the higher rate was £3,213, in this case there is a deficit of £3,823.

These examples illustrate why discounted cash flow methods have become popular as with a relatively simple method of layout a great number of variables can be built into calculations without too much drudgery, the electronic calculator making the calculations easy. Other variables can be included as appropriate and these can include allowances for sinking funds and for tax liabilities.

Discounted cash flow calculations more easily permit the cost of outgoings to be calculated at the precise time they are likely to occur, rather than assuming, as is generally the case in the conventional investment valuation, that all outgoings will occur at the ends of the relevant years. Tax or rate liabilities in particular may be phased over a period of time rather than being payable at one specific date, and such phasing can be incorporated in a discounted cash flow calculation so that more precise estimates of the discounted burden of future liabilities are made.

The approach sets out clearly on paper the various outflows and inflows and the discounting calculations, and it enables easy comparison to be made between alternatives. All these variables could be incorporated into the conventional valuation format, although probably not with such ease or such clarity for comparison purposes.

Valuation using the Net Present Value Method

The above examples have illustrated the use of the method for analysis. The purchase price and costs have been known and have been incorporated in the overall analysis of the investment.

When a valuation is made the purchase price and costs are not known; to find them is the object of the exercise. The Net Present Value method can be used just as easily as a method of valuation. This is done by omitting the purchase price and costs of acquisition and then taking the balance of the discounted net inflow and net outflow figures for the years concerned. This balance will give the figure which one can afford to pay for a property at a given rate of interest. Considering Examples 3 to 6 as methods of valuation:

In Example 3 Property A at 12% is valued at £118,570,
In Example 4 Property A at 16% is valued at £104,787,
In Example 5 Property B at 12% is valued at £96,370, and
In Example 6 Property B at 16% is valued at £85,177.

These figures represent the values placed on the expected future net returns from the properties at the given target rates. They therefore represent the maximum figures (inclusive of purchase costs) which potential purchasers should be prepared to bid unless they revise their valuations for some valid reason.

Potential purchasers would only bid up to these maximum figures if the pressures of the market forced them to do so, and they would purchase at lower figures if possible.

General Comments on Net Present Value Method

The method permits a more sophisticated treatment of investment valuations than does the traditional approach, but it is only as good as the person using it. It can be very accurate, but it can also be very inaccurate, and the degree of accuracy will depend upon the accuracy of the various inputs.

It has the virtue of enabling many relevant items to be included in the calculations in a format which allows ease of understanding, and the same calculation can be used both for valuation and comparison. It also forces the valuer to give individual consideration to a number of factors which are considered collectively when using the traditional method of valuation.

The net present value approach shows whether an investment is expected to be viable or not, and it predicts the size of the profit or loss, but it does not give a precise indication of the rate at which an investment will earn money.

The Internal Rate of Return

This is the other discounted cash flow method which will be considered and its objective is to show the rate at which an investment earns money.

The only indication the Net Present Value method gave of the rate at which money was earned was to show whether the rate of earning was below or above the rate chosen for the calculations (that is the target rate). To know the size of a profit (or a loss) may be helpful, but if the highest return also requires the highest capital outlay the information may be of limited use. An investor's real wish will be to know the rate at which his capital will earn money. The Internal Rate of Return method therefore seeks to find the precise rate at which the capital invested will earn money thus enabling a more precise comparison to be made between competing investment opportunities.

The rate of interest at which the net present value of the outflows and the net present value of the inflows are equal will be the rate at which an investment earns money. Because the Internal Rate of Return reveals the earning power of money it not only permits comparison between different property investments, but it also allows comparison to be made with other types of investment, such as gilt edge stock and equities.

The Internal Rate of Return is in fact found by trial and error. In Example 3 at a target rate of 12% a surplus of £10,570 could be expected, whilst in Example 4 the use of the target rate of 16% for the same investment revealed an expected deficit of £3,213. Somewhere between 12% and 16% there must therefore be a point at which discounted outflows and inflows are exactly equal and that rate of interest will be the Internal Rate of Return.

By interpolation we can anticipate that the Internal Rate of Return will be about 15%, and we can then make calculations to check the precise rate.

Example 7
The facts are as in Examples 3 and 4 but the objective is to find the Internal Rate of Return.

End of Year	Particulars	Outflow	Inflow	Net Flow + or −	PV of £1 @15%	Net Outflow	Net Inflow
0	Purchase Price	100,000					
	Purchase Costs	8,000		−108,000	1	108,000	
1	Rent		11,000	+11,000	·8695652		9,565
2	Rent		11,000	+11,000	·7561437		8,318
3	Rent		11,000	+11,000	·6575162		7,233
4	Rent		11,000				
	Sale Proceeds		140,000				
	Sale Costs	6,000		+145,000	·5717532		82,904
						108,000	108,020

Net Present Value 20

At a discount rate of 15% the discounted net outflows and net inflows are almost equal, and it can be seen that the Internal Rate of Return of the investment is therefore 15%. It would be possible to work out the precise rate at which the two columns are equal, but for most purposes the rate of 15% would be sufficiently accurate.

A Comparison of the Net Present Value and Internal Rate of Return Methods

In the Net Present Value method one rate of interest is chosen (the target rate) to find whether an investment is profitable at that rate. Because of this the method is simple involving no real mathematical difficulties. The method is particularly suitable for valuation, and the only real problem is the choice of the target rate. This could be determined by the cost of borrowing, the opportunity cost of money or the risk rating of the particular investment.

In the Internal Rate of Return method calculations have to be made at a number of different rates of interest to determine the actual earning power of an investment. More calculations are therefore involved but with modern programmable calculators this really poses no problem. Whereas the Net Present Value method only gives the size of an excess or a deficit, the Internal Rate of Return method reveals the earning power of an investment and this makes the method more suitable for the analysis of investments and for comparison purposes.

General

Discounted cash flow techniques do not conflict with traditional investment valuation methods; rather do they represent a development and refinement of the same basic principles used in the traditional approach. Their use will not necessarily give better or more accurate results, as much will depend upon the skill and judgement of the person doing the calculations, the results obtained from the calculations being very much dependent upon the various assumptions made by the user.

However, it is probably true to say that where a calculation or valuation is dependent upon a considerable number of variables and a large number or varying pattern of time periods, the use of discounted cash flow techniques is more appropriate than the traditional investment valuation approach. It is also easy to incorporate in discounted cash flow calculations estimates to reflect the effect of inflation upon future income flows and outgoings. Likewise, whereas traditional methods cannot easily reflect the possibility of the future sale of the income producing asset at an enhanced value, such a calculation is easily incorporated in a discounted cash flow calculation. (The reader should not overlook the fact that it may in some instances be necessary to allow for future decreases in income or value.) In this respect discounted cash flow techniques are particularly useful as they facilitate the estimation of a true return over time allowing for changes in value and liabilities over the time period. The traditional valuation approach generally assumes a rate of return and utilises estimates of returns and liabilities at figures appropriate at the time the valuation is made, and consequently is not likely to give an indication of the true return to an asset over the period of ownership.

CHAPTER 20

THE EFFECT OF STATUTES

Valuations so far have been discussed taking into account what might be termed the normal market factors which affect value. These include the physical features of a property, geographical features, the legal interests and liabilities, and finance and the economy generally. There may, however, be somewhat abnormal factors introduced, in that governments pass Statutes, or Acts of Parliament as they are more often described, which may interfere with normal market conditions.

The passing of an Act may suddenly create completely new conditions from those which previously existed. It may introduce factors which could not previously have been foreseen, and the property market may be taken completely by surprise. In such circumstances the passing of an Act of Parliament may have an immediate effect on the market, resulting from the new conditions suddenly imposed. However, if the market has been awakened to the possibility of a particular Act of Parliament some time before it is actually drafted in Bill form, it may have anticipated the effects of such an Act, and the passing into law of the Bill may have a less marked effect on market values than would otherwise have been the case.

Indeed, the market may possibly have over-reacted to the promise of a particular piece of legislation, and on the publication of a Bill it could be that values rise rather than fall, because its implications may not be as severe as the market had previously feared.

Whatever the effects may be, large or small, immediate or gradual, it is the valuer's role to interpret the implications of Statutes and try to calculate in money terms the changes in value which may result.

It is not intended in this book to discuss any Acts of Parliament in detail. Such is the task of an advanced text-book on valuations and can only be done effectively after a student has attained a relatively high technical standard and has a reasonable legal grounding. At this stage all that will be done is to discuss in very general detail the effect on market values of the passing of Acts of Parliament, and the valuer's role in attempting to assess such effects.

Governments pass Statutes for a wide variety of reasons; some are passed for tax-raising purposes and may have a direct impact on the values of investment properties if they reduce the net of tax income produced; some are passed to affect the legal relationships between different people or organisations, and may affect property values if they affect the bargaining powers of the parties to a transaction; some are passed to enable public bodies to compulsorily acquire property owned by others and such powers may have a considerable effect on both the use and value of property.

Statutes may relate to all properties, or they may relate to a specific class of property. Indeed, they may not necessarily relate to property at all but may nevertheless have an important impact on the property market if they have an effect on investors and their general approach to investment. An example of the type of legislation which affects all properties is planning legislation which often imposes quite rigid control on the development and use of land. Such legislation therefore has an effect on the value of any piece of land, in that the freedom to use it as the owner may wish, may be withdrawn, and he may only be able to use it for a particular purpose if the planning authority deems it appropriate to grant permission for such use. The power of an authority to refuse permission for certain uses or, alternatively, to grant permission, can create situations in which an acre of land could be worth perhaps, £2,500 for agricultural purposes or, alternatively, £100,000 or more for development.

If a planning authority will not permit property to be put to its most valuable use, then its value must inevitably be lower than if the higher and more valuable use were allowed. A typical example of such a situation may arise with residential property which could easily be used for prestige office accommodation were planning permission given, but for which the local planning authority are unwilling to grant a permission. The property is thereby restricted to residential user, for which purposes it may be very much less valuable than if office use were permitted. The valuer will be able to assess this lower market value relatively easily in most cases by consulting his office records and by using his knowledge of the area.

Other Statutes may affect specific types of property only, and there are numerous instances of such legislation in the United Kingdom. Business properties have for many years been affected by the Landlord and Tenant Acts of 1927 and 1954 and related legislation, whilst the various Factory Acts are examples of a type of legislation which affects only a restricted class of business properties. Agricultural properties are directly affected by the Agricultural Holdings Act 1948, the Agricultural Act 1958 and several other more recent Statutes. Residential properties have since the First World War been affected by a whole series of Rent Acts, the Leasehold Reform Act 1967, various Housing Acts and other Statutes.

There are many other Statutes which affect property values, but mention of just these few will suffice to show the reader that the valuer has much legislation to contend with.

The passing of an Act of Parliament, or indeed the publication of a Bill, may have an immediate effect on the market, or possibly a more gradual effect. A gradual effect may occur if an Act provides for the introduction of new provisions affecting properties, and these provisions are phased to come into effect at a number of future dates. As the various provisions become operative, so the Act has a greater impact and in consequence more effect on values.

Alternatively the effect of a Statute may be restricted in that its provisions may affect only a few properties in a particular category. A Housing Act may affect only certain types of residential property, and generally the types affected will be those less fit for human habitation. It might well be that a particular Housing Act referred only to properties of a certain number of storeys, or in a certain area. The scope of the provisions and the type of property which they affect will generally be self-evident on reading an Act.

It is the valuer's task to interpret the provisions of each Statute, and the only way to do this correctly is to take up the Statute and read it. This may seem an obvious suggestion but often it is all too easy to refer to a text-book written by a specialist on the subject, and to rely upon this source of information rather than referring directly to the Act. Any who adopt this course do so at their own peril, because in doing so they are placing their faith in the wisdom and skill of the writer. There is no doubt much to be gained from reading such text-books and treatises, but this should be done not to the exclusion of an inspection of the Statute but rather to broaden one's outlook and at the same time get another opinion on the interpretation of what is often far from clear-cut legislation.

Having read and interpreted the various provisions of a Statute, the next step is to decide which provisions are important in the valuation process. The valuer may decide either that he must vary the method of valuation he uses or the figures used in his valuation. Either of these approaches, or possibly a combination of the two, may enable him to take account of the provisions of a Statute and reflect their effect on value.

Statutes vary considerably in that they may have what can

be described as either a direct effect on value or an indirect effect. The direct effect may arise in cases in which a Statute states that a specific valuation approach is to be used in particular circumstances. An example of one which did this was the Land Commission Act 1967, which laid out in very detailed form the various valuation approaches to be used in calculating the development value of a property, on which betterment levy would be charged. Likewise, the Leasehold Reform Act 1967 introduced provisions relating to residential properties held on long leases at low rents. It specified the valuation approach to be used in calculating the sum to be paid by a long leaseholder who claimed the right to purchase the freehold interest in his house from the freeholder. Both these Acts had a direct effect on the valuation approach to be used.

An Act may have a direct effect on the market in that certain properties may be removed from the market because it has been passed, and this affects both the value of the properties so removed and the value of the properties remaining in the market, as they may well become more valuable because the total supply has been reduced by the passing of the Statute.

An indirect effect of the passing of a Statute may be that the underlying conditions of the market are altered by its introduction. Landlord and tenant relations have been altered in the past in a wide range of properties by the introduction of such Acts as the Agricultural Holdings Act 1948, and the Landlord and Tenant Act 1954, the latter Act affecting the landlord and tenant relations in both residential properties and business properties. An alteration in the rights of landlord and tenant has an effect on value in that there is a tendency for the value of one party's interest to be decreased whilst the value of the other party's interest increases. The extent of such increases and decreases will vary, depending upon how far-reaching the provisions of an Act are, and how the normal bargaining positions of the parties are affected by it. In some cases the variation may be in a form which does not necessarily have a marked effect on the value of a property. However, the converse often seems to apply.

The Rent Act 1957 is an example of an Act which had a profound effect on the value of certain types of property. Prior to its passing a very large proportion of the unfurnished rented accommodation in this country was controlled, and the tenants were enjoying very great security of tenure with rents fixed at levels which the landlord could not exceed without breaking the law. The 1957 Act removed certain types of residential property from these controls, but others remained within the system of control. Those that remained within control were subject to stringent conditions regarding the rent which could be charged. This was assessed by reference to the gross values of the property in 1956, and rough and ready as such a method of rent assessment was in 1957 when the Act was passed, with the passage of time the method and the level of rent charged became even more rough and ready, to the extent of being positively ludicrous. Rents on many properties which remained controlled stayed at basically the same level for periods in excess of twenty years with the result that the income to a landlord was often so low that it was quite impossible for properties to be maintained in a reasonable state of repair. Even where the income exceeded the outgoings, and there were many instances where the reverse was the case, the general level of net income arising from such properties was so low that they became more and more unattractive as investments and changed hands at figures which, in comparison with the vacant possession value of similar properties, were incredibly low. The 1957 Act therefore had a great effect on the value of those properties which remained controlled under its provisions, and their values related more to 1957 values than to the comparable values of residential properties which escaped control under the Act. The effect of this Act on residential property values was both obvious and considerable.

A valuer may often encounter a different type of problem arising from the existence of a Statute, in that it may effectively destroy the open market for a particular type of property. The Leasehold Reform Act 1967 gave to certain long leaseholders of residential properties the right to buy the freeholds of their homes from the freeholders, and the very existence of these provisions has virtually destroyed the market for long leaseholds in many sectors of the residential market. A valuer consequently finds that he has to attempt to assess value under the terms of the Act without in many cases there being any current evidence of the value of such interests. He is in the position of having to estimate market value on a hypothetical basis, which creates many difficulties and leaves many doubts at the end of the exercise. In such circumstances he can do little more than make an honest assessment of what he considers value under the terms of the Act to be, but he will rarely be able to argue to uphold the value he assesses in such conditions with as much conviction as he could do if he were assessing a value in normal open market conditions.

A somewhat similar situation arises when property is compulsorily acquired. There are several Acts of Parliament which may affect the basis of valuation in such circumstances, but in most cases the main code of compensation will be that contained in the Land Compensation Act 1961. This Act details various provisions under which an acquiring authority has to assess the compensation payable to the owner of any interest in land which is compulsorily acquired by them. The basic figure which has to be paid is the value of an interest as if it were offered for sale in the open market by a willing seller. There are many other provisions contained in the Act, all intended to clarify the valuation approach to be used in any situation, but their general effect is that an owner whose interest has been compulsorily acquired shall be paid sufficient money to put him in an equivalent financial position after the acquisition to that he was in prior to the acquisition. He is to be reimbursed for all losses which are a direct result of his property being taken.

On paper and in theory this proposition is quite straightforward and very fair; but to put it into practice may be far from simple. The mere hint of a possible compulsory acquisition may immediately kill any potential market for the property involved. It may be that several properties are to be compulsorily acquired, or indeed a whole area of a town. No matter how many properties are involved, it is almost inevitable that the time lapse from the first mention of a scheme until its final implementation, when the properties are compulsorily acquired, will be several years, possibly even many years. Because of the long time between the inception of the scheme and its completion, it may be that there are no market transactions whatsoever in a particular area for a period of several years, as, whenever an affected property is offered for sale on the market, would-be purchasers are scared away on learning of the impending compulsory acquisition. A valuer may therefore find himself in the position of having to assess a value for open market purposes in an area where there have been no open market transactions for several years. Even if there have been some transactions in the area, they may have taken place at considerably lower figures than would have been the case but for the threat of compulsory acquisition.

It may be that a landowner has been put into the position of having to dispose of a property and yet has been unable to force the acquiring authority to purchase his interest. Such a situation might arise if property has to be sold to pay taxes due following a death and the inheritor of the property is left with the choice of either holding on to it and borrowing money to pay the tax or selling the blighted property at a figure well below the normal market value. The latter may be the most expeditious course of action open to him, but the sale on the open market of a blighted property may create a low tone of values, and an unrealistically low base for assessing the compensation payable on other affected properties.

There may be several courses open to a valuer in his attempts to find the true market value, that is the value ignoring depreciation caused by the threat of compulsory acquisition. He may attempt to relate other areas which are not affected by the threat to the area with which he is dealing. He may look at the evidence of such areas and calculate that values have risen by certain percentages since the compulsory acquisition was first suggested. He may then attempt to up-date the values in the affected area by using graphs projecting the values in existence at the date the scheme was first announced in an effort to relate them to the current market.

Such projections would assume that the values of the property with which he is dealing would have increased at the same rate as properties in other areas over the same period. This is a valid approach to the problem but it does not necessarily prove anything—it merely suggests what might have been.

In attempting such an exercise a valuer must pay great attention to all the other factors which could have affected the market in the area, for it may be that, even without the threat of compulsory acquisition, values in a certain area might have decreased. In circumstances in which properties are to be acquired for the construction of a dual carriageway road, traffic in the area may have become so bad that the existing single carriageway road is quite inadequate to cope with it, and the area is being harmed considerably by the excess traffic. Had there been no road scheme the area would have deteriorated because of the adverse traffic conditions. If this were the case a valuer would have to isolate the depreciation which would have occurred in any event, from the total depreciation, the balance being the depreciation in value which results from the threat of compulsory acquisition. It is not difficult to foresee the problems in such an exercise. A valuer can at best believe that the figure he puts forward is reasonable, rather than believe it is the only acceptable figure.

Another way of trying to assess what open market value would have been but for the threat of compulsory acquisition might be to look at the market trend in the area prior to the first threat of acquisition, and to project the previous trends in value forward from that date on the assumption that they would have continued along the same pattern as before. Subject to the type of reservation outlined in the previous paragraph, this might be an acceptable solution.

Yet another attempt to solve the same problem might be to look at any properties within the area concerned which have

not been adversely affected by the threat of compulsory acquisition, in cases where only certain classes of property are affected.
This may be an easier situation for the valuer to deal with, and
it may be perfectly reasonable to assume that values in the
properties affected by acquisition would have moved similarly
to those of properties not affected. Here again, though, there
are serious reservations, as it may be that the different types
of property are so different that their markets are completely
dissimilar and subject to different factors where value is concerned.

It is not difficult to see the problems facing a valuer when
legislation effectively destroys the market, and much will depend
on his judgment and his interpretation of the various statutes
if he is to obtain a reasonably correct answer. Two equally con-
scientious and skilled valuers, one working for an acquiring authority, the other working for a claimant, may arrive at quite
different answers concerning the same piece of property.
Although a layman might consider this to be unreasonable, it
is only fair to point out that in any situation which involves
judgment a difference of opinion of this nature is likely to arise.
Two barristers may consider the same case and each reach a
different conclusion, just as two doctors may each inspect a
patient and recommend different cures for the same ailment.
Where facts are uncertain it is almost inevitable that there will
be differences of opinion between people, but the role of a valuer
in this type of situation will be to use his technical knowledge,
his skill at interpreting statutes, and his experience and judgment
in an attempt to reach as nearly as possible the correct valuation.

A more general type of statute which may affect values is the
various Finance Acts. Indeed a Budget itself may do so, the
Finance Act coming later and confirming the promises made
in the Budget. The availability of credit and the cost of credit
is an important element in any form of investment, and is as
important with property investment as with any other investment. Promises or threats contained within a Budget may affect
the thinking of investors and influence their subsequent actions.
The Budget may encourage investment, or it may equally well
discourage it. If it encourages investment, it may encourage it
in particular forms while discouraging it in others. It may cause
a particular form of investment to be relatively more attractive
than others, even when the general effect of the Budget has
been to encourage all types of investment.

If new taxes are promised or threatened, such as Development
Gains Tax, Development Land Tax, Wealth Tax and Capital
Transfer Tax, the reaction of investors may be to wait and see

the precise content of the detailed legislation before embarking on any new projects. There may be many reasons why an investor will wait and see. It may be that he merely wishes to see which investments will be most attractive after the new measures are put into effect, and then to invest in those particular investments, or alternatively, it may be that the investor waits to see whether any form of investment is likely to be worthwhile, or whether immediate consumption will be more beneficial to him than saving and investment.

There are many possibilities and a valuer has to look at Budgetary announcements and endeavour to assess what effect they will have on the investment market generally. Here again much skill will be required, but as a professional man the valuer will have to commit himself to a certain extent and make predictions of what he thinks will happen and what the effect will be on property values.

Many hours of study are required to understand fully the effect of statutes and government action on property values, but it is hoped that this brief look at the problem will have alerted the would-be valuer to the problems he will have to face. They should not deter him, as these are the very factors which help to make the whole science or art of valuation intriguing and interesting. To summarise, the valuer has to be adept at understanding Acts of Parliament, and he has to be able to isolate the important factors affecting property values. He has to understand their effect and then be sufficiently competent in the mathematical process to vary his normal valuation procedure to take account of the new circumstances resulting from an Act. He has to be analytical, practical and methodical, and, needless to say, experience will be very useful to him in this task. A good knowledge of people and an understanding of the way they think and the way they react to various situations are also very useful, as the market for property, like any other market, is made up of people. To understand people is to a large extent to understand values.

CHAPTER 21

TAXATION AND PROPERTY INVESTMENT

Earlier in this book tax was mentioned and its effect on sinking funds was discussed. Calculations were made and it was shown how simple adjustments could be made to allow for the payment of income-tax on sinking fund allotments. The question whether yields should be considered gross-of-tax or net-of-tax was also examined, and it was pointed out that as yields on most other investments were normally considered on a gross basis and different taxpayers had different tax liabilities it was convenient to consider yields from property on a gross basis. Because of the multiplicity of tax liabilities, no single adjustment for tax would be appropriate to all potential investors and, indeed, an adjustment at the standard rate might, in reality, be applicable to no one.

However, the effect of tax is very important when investment is considered, and this importance tends to grow each year with the growing complexity of tax systems. Although income earners normally compare gross salaries when comparing the merits of different jobs, it is nevertheless probably true that once employed in a particular job the majority are more interested in their net salary, as it is the amount of money available to them after payment of tax which dictates their standard of living. The net income available from property investment must inevitably be very important to an investor as it is pointless considering the gross income if, after tax has been deducted, the remaining sum bears no relationship to the original income-flow. The investor cannot spend the tax element of his income, and it seems logical that his real interest should lie in considering the income available for his personal use.

This concept may appear contrary to the conventions of property valuation, but if attention is given only to the gross yield before payment of tax the investor is in fact considering the combined yield which the property gives to him and the Revenue. The amount that the Revenue receives is hardly beneficial to him, and it therefore seems more appropriate to consider the net-of-tax value of a particular investment to him personally. As yields in the market are normally quoted gross-of-tax, it would therefore appear that two valuations at least should be done for almost every market appraisal. A valuation at a gross-of-tax rate may be appropriate to discover what the market will be prepared to pay for a property, and a net-of-tax valuation will endeavour to find the figure which the particular investor can afford to pay. The two figures may well be quite different, and if the investor's personal net-of-tax valuation proves to be lower than the normal market valuation then it is probably because he is in a less advantageous position after tax than others in the market.

As there is a multiplicity of tax rates applicable to different investors, depending upon their personal circumstances, it may be that income-tax liability for different investors will vary considerably, particularly as U.K. tax on income ranged, for example, in 1987–88 from a basic rate of 27% to 60%. The tax liability of companies is on a different basis, and corporation tax might be chargeable to small companies at 27%, or to large companies at 35%.

Tax structures often reveal considerable differences between individuals and, indeed, between individuals and companies, and a person might decide that his activities would be better carried on by a company than by him as an individual, as a lower tax liability might be incurred by a company than he personally would incur. There would be many other considerations to take into account, however, before reaching such a decision.

Not only income and corporation tax, but taxes on capital gains and the development value of land may also be of concern to a property owner. U.K. capital gains tax is levied at a rate of 30% on any gain realised but as at 1987–88 gains not exceeding £6,600 in any year of assessment are not charged to the tax.

If a capital gain is made there could therefore be a low tax liability on that gain so that if a highly taxed person has property investments, it may well be better for him to attempt to make capital gains which will be taxed at 30% than for him to receive income which will be taxed at 60%. It is therefore important for him to consider different courses of action and to decide what his total tax liability is likely to be in each case, and then to choose the course of action which leaves him in the best financial situation after all his tax liabilities have been met.

There have been a number of different taxes on the development value of land in the United Kingdom since the Second World War, the most recent having been Development Land Tax.

There were some exclusions from this tax, including the first element of development value realised in any financial year, the amount exempt having varied from time to time. An individual who was in a position to realise development value in excess of the exempt amount should therefore have considered whether it might not have been advisable to sell his properties in different years in order to restrict the development value realised in any year to the exempt sum. In subsequent years advantage could again be taken of the exemption. By adopting such a policy the vendor might well escape tax liability completely, and the consequent tax saving may well have more than repaid the waiting. Tax planning of this nature can be a very important activity for the property owner or property adviser.

Taxes which become due at the transfer of property on death have varied considerably in the United Kingdom since the early 1970's, "death duties" having existed at various times in the form of Estate Duty, Capital Transfer Tax and now Inheritance Tax, each with a range of tax levels which vary with the total value of the property transferred. In addition, variations in the details of each tax from time to time have resulted in constantly changing liabilities for a given value depending upon the precise date of death.

Some other countries have tax systems which levy tax on transfer at death, and where there is such a tax the valuer may often have to assess the tax due on the transfer of property interests both freehold and leasehold. In some cases it will be necessary to make such assessments even where death has not occurred in order to assess the contingent tax liability which would arise should the property owner die. Such a valuation could, for instance, be needed for insurance purposes to provide for an insurance payment to cover the cost of Inheritance Tax (in the U.K.) when it occurs.

Such taxes are often quite complex and will not be discussed in detail here, but it is worth noting that following the U.K. 1987 Budget Inheritance Tax on transfers after 18th March 1987 can range from Nil, to a rate of 30% (or 15% for transfers during a lifetime) to a top rate of 60%. Because of the "banding" of liability and the fact that some elements of any estate will be taxed at less than 60% the maximum average rate of Inheritance Tax will in fact always be something less than 60%.

When new taxes are introduced or changes are made to existing taxes, investors have to consider their effect on their investments and when the full implications are known investment policies need to be adjusted to give the most advantageous net-of-tax position. This is yet another consideration for the taxpayer or the investor to take into account, and there is little doubt that for many years past policy decisions by investors have been very much influenced by tax considerations.

A number of relatively simple examples follow to illustrate some considerations which an investor might have to take into account in formulating policy. The first example concerns an investor who is faced with the decision as to whether he should sell an asset and re-invest his money in an alternative investment. In many cases if the tax liability is ignored there will be little doubt that an investor would be well advised to sell his current investment and divert his funds elsewhere, but because the liability to capital gains tax on any gain he makes will reduce the net amount available for re-investment, he may well be encouraged to retain the current but inferior investment rather than sell it.

Readers should note that these examples are given to illustrate the effect that tax considerations may have on investment decisions. Rules and rates of tax used are those appropriate at the date of writing (which precedes the date of publication) and both may vary with the passage of time. These rules and rates should not therefore be used by readers for tax calculations but those current at the time should be checked by reference to an up-to-date tax encyclopaedia.

Example 1

An investor owns a property which he bought in 1968 for which the indexed purchase price is £15,000 and which gives an annual income before tax of £18,000 per annum. He has been offered £180,000 by the lessee, who would like to purchase the freehold. The investor would like to accept the offer as he is of advancing years and the management of the property is proving troublesome to him, it being situated 200 miles from where he lives. He would like to acquire another investment nearer his home and has asked you to advise him. You are aware that he pays income-tax at 45%.

Present Income: This shows a 10% yield on the capital value.

Income net of outgoings	£ 18,000 p.a.
Less Income-tax at 45%	£ 8,100
Income available for spending	£ 9,900

Proceeds of sale on suggested terms

Sale proceeds net of expenses, say	£174,000
Less Total purchase costs, say	£ 15,300
Capital Gain	£158,700

Capital gains tax liability 158,700 × 30% = £47,610

The sum available for re-investment amounts to the net sale proceeds of £174,000 less capital gains tax of £47,610 or £126,390. If the freeholder could re-invest all this money in a similar risk property he would get a 10% yield or an annual income of £12,639 before the payment of income-tax. The tax payable on this income at 45% would be £5687·55 and his annual income after tax would therefore be £6951·45 or £2948·55 per annum less than his current income.

As a result, although both he and the lessee would otherwise like to do a deal, the potential liability to capital gains tax means that the investor cannot afford to proceed with a sale unless he can re-invest in a property with an anticipated early growth in income. The incidence of capital gains tax will therefore force him to reject a course of action which in all other respects would be advisable.

Alternatively, where on property management and investment management grounds, the retention and leasing of a property might be advisable, a high liability to tax, particularly at the top rate of income-tax may make retention so unprofitable after the payment of tax that the investor may decide on tax grounds alone to sell the property.

Example 2

A business man purchased a property in 1966 at an indexed purchase price of £20,000 and it now has a market value of £160,000. He would like to dispose of his business and retire, and he has offered his manager the property at market value. The manager is unable to raise the necessary capital and has offered to rent it at £16,000 per annum. The business man pays tax at 60%.

Position if property is let to the manager

Annual income	£ 16,000
Tax at 60%	£ 9,600
Balance available after tax	£ 6,400 p.a.

This is equivalent to a return of 4% on the market value.

Position if property is sold to a third party

Net sale proceeds, say	£155,000
Less total purchase costs	£ 20,500
Capital gain	£134,500
Capital Gains Tax at 30% × 134,500 = £40,350	

The net sum available to the businessman would equal:

Net sale proceeds	£155,000
Less tax	£ 40,350
	£114,650

Analysis of net gain on original purchase

Net of tax proceeds of sale	£114,650
Original expenditure	£ 20,500
Net gain	£ 94,150

This is equivalent to a net of tax yield of about 8% per annum over a period of ownership of 22 years.

Rather than accept a net-of-tax rent of £6,400 per annum, which is a net yield of about 4%, even though he would like to assist his manager, the business man would be better advised to sell the property and to re-invest his money in a way in which he stands a chance of making another capital gain which will show him the equivalent of a 8% p.a. net of tax yield.

If his liability to income-tax were only 45% the position would be as follows:

Annual income	£16,000
Income tax at 45%	£ 7,200
Income net-of-tax	£ 8,800

This gives a yield of 5·5% on the market value, which considerably narrows the gap between the two alternatives. If income-tax was only 30% the net-of-tax yield on letting would be 7% and the business man would be able to assist his manager without himself losing much financially.

The previous two examples have considered one individual and his decisions regarding future investment policy, but there will also be situations in which two individuals looking at the same investment will reach completely different decisions simply because they have differing liabilities to tax. An investment which is attractive to a man paying income-tax at 30% may be far from attractive to one whose tax liability on income is 60%.

Example 3

A leasehold property yields a gross-of-tax income of £20,000 per annum and to provide for the recoupment of capital an annual sinking fund of £4,000 per annum is required.

The investor with a tax liability of 27% will be in the following position

Gross-of-tax income	£20,000
Less income tax	£ 5,400
Net-of-tax income	£14,600

The net-of-tax income will comprise

(1) Spendable Income	£10,600
(2) Annual Sinking Fund	£ 4,000

An alternative way of looking at these calculations is:

Gross-of-tax income	£20,000
ASF required after tax	£ 4,000

If the sinking fund is enlarged to allow for income tax liability on it, it becomes:

$$\text{Net ASF} \times \frac{100}{100 - 27} = £4,000 \times \frac{100}{73} = £5,479{\cdot}45$$

Gross-of-Tax Spendable Income = Total Income—Grossed Up
Sinking Fund = £20,000 − £5,479·45 = £14,520·55

The net-of-tax amounts would be:

Gross Spendable Income	£14,520·55
Less Tax at 27%	3,920·55
Net-of-tax spendable income	£10,600·00
Gross Sinking Fund	£ 5,479·45
Less Tax at 27%	£ 1,479·45
Net-of-tax sinking fund	£ 4,000·00

From the point of view of the taxpayer paying income-tax at 60% the alternative calculations would be as follows:

Annual sinking Fund after tax   £4,000

$$\text{Grossed up Annual Sinking Fund} = 4,000 \times \frac{100}{100 - 60} = 4,000 \times \frac{100}{40}$$

$$= £10,000$$

This is a large sum compared with the total annual income of £20,000. An investor with a high tax liability would therefore have to consider very carefully whether the purchase of such an investment was advisable in view of the large amount of total income which would be monopolised by the tax liability on the sinking fund.

Indeed, in the past total tax liability on such investments could have been as high as 98% in which case the calculations would have been:—

Annual sinking fund after tax   £4,000

$$\text{Grossed up Annual Sinking Fund} = 4,000 \times \frac{100}{100 - 98} = 4,000 \times \frac{100}{2}$$

$$= £200,000$$

Obviously, investors who had tax liabilities of 98% could not even have contemplated the possibility of purchasing an interest in which the tax liability resulted in the grossed up annual sinking fund requirement being ten times the gross of tax annual income produced by the investment.

Our original taxpayer, however, retained 53% of the gross income as spendable income after paying income-tax and after providing for a sinking fund to recoup his capital.

The above example illustrates a situation in which the individuals have widely different tax liabilities, but there will be many cases in which a marginally more favourable tax position for one investor will result in his being able to outbid another potential investor who is more heavily taxed.

The examples have purposely been kept both few and simple, and it is not the intention of the author to become involved with teaching tax, nor to get involved in complicated calculations which are better left until the student has got a thorough grasp of basic valuation principles and is able to understand most of the implications of property investment. The main objective at this stage is simply to illustrate the fact that the existence of different rates of tax and the resultant different tax liabilities (which may vary dependent upon the decisions an individual investor takes), are factors which must inevitably have a great effect on policy decisions. Indeed, the importance of such considerations is so great that tax planning is an important science in these days. The person who fully understands all the implications of complicated tax systems, if there is such a person, is worth his weight in gold to an investor and, indeed, is able to command high fees if able to give quality advice.

CHAPTER 22

FINANCE AND GEARING

Obviously, before an investor can contemplate purchasing a property interest, he must have the necessary money, and a relatively large sum will be required, for even the purchase of a small property will probably cost in the region of £50,000. Larger properties will cost many times more, and some cost many millions of pounds to purchase. Because of the need for such large sums, the majority of purchasers cannot provide all the necessary money from their own funds, and they have to borrow to obtain sufficient money to proceed with a purchase.

This raises the problem of finding where money can be borrowed, and as the type of property varies, so the source of finance may vary. Irrespective of the source of finance, the better the terms the borrower can arrange, the more beneficial the overall property investment is likely to prove. If an investor is able to borrow a substantial sum of money at a relatively low rate of interest and is able to ensure that the money will be available to him for a long period, the overall security of his investment is likely to be considerably stronger than if he were only able to borrow at a high rate of interest for a short time. The terms on which an investor can borrow will depend not only on the type of investment, but also upon the general state of the economy (local, national and international), at the time he is borrowing. If overall interest rates are high then the cost of borrowing is likely to be high, whereas during times of low interest rates, he will naturally have a greater chance of borrowing money on attractive terms.

Other critical factors influencing the terms upon which a borrower can obtain money are the reputation, character and standing of the borrower himself. A person of proven character and ability is far more likely to be able to borrow on good terms than one of doubtful character who has no previous dealings in the field into which he wishes to venture. There is nothing particularly surprising or unreasonable about such a state of affairs. It would be a foolish man who would offer as favourable terms to a completely unknown individual as he would to a person of proven ability. The more reputable and established an investor becomes in his particular line of business, the more preferential the terms he is likely to obtain.

As far as the type of property is concerned, the borrowing sources can be split into two basic markets; the market for residential property finance, and that for commercial property finance.

For many years in the United Kingdom the chief source of finance for the purchase of residential property has been, and still is, the Building Society movement. Loans from this source have normally only been obtainable for the purchase of residential properties for the borrower's own use, Societies rarely lending money to finance the purchase of residential properties for investment purposes or for the purchase of commercial properties. Funds may occasionally have been provided for the purchase of a property with a mixed residential and retail or commercial use if the property was being bought for the purchaser's own use. Building Society loans have in general, provided an incredibly cheap form of borrowing at rates of interest which have normally been much lower than those charged on loans for the purchase of non-residential property. Additionally, in the United Kingdom borrowers of funds for the purchase of a house for their own use, have for many years been able to get substantial income tax relief on interest payments which has further reduced the cost of purchasing a home.

During the 1980's the British building societies have expanded into other areas of activity such as the provision of banking services, and changes to the legislation under which they operate now enable them to become involved in activities previously denied to them. Despite these developments there is little reason to suspect they will not continue to be the major source of funds for house purchase.

There are several reasons why the rate of interest charged by building societies is low, a major one undoubtedly being the fact that traditionally building societies have not been profit-making bodies. Their objective is to provide money for house-purchase, and they do so by borrowing from savers who wish to deposit money in a safe investment from which it can be readily withdrawn if needed.

This money is then lent to others who wish to purchase houses. Societies borrow money at a lower rate of interest than the rate they charge on their loans, but the difference between these rates of interest is not intended to provide them with a profit, merely to cover their operating costs. Although there appear to have been some extravagances in the building societies movement in recent years, in that a multiplicity of offices owned by a multiplicity of competing societies seem to have been opened, it is a fact that their overall operating costs are in general very low, and this has helped to enable them to offer funds to the public at low rates of interest. The borrower who considers that their rates of interest are not low merely needs to investigate the commercial money market to persuade himself otherwise.

There are also other reasons why the rates charged by building societies are relatively low. Whatever may be the state of the economy, people will always require houses in which to live, and so, although a depressed house market may exist in times of depression in the economy, the market for houses is not likely to disappear completely. There is consequently always a market for residential property, even though prices may at times fall. However, the record over the post-war period is of steadily increasing house prices in spite of periodic depressions, so the security of a loan made by a Building Society is, generally speaking, increasing over time, rather than decreasing or staying static.

The risk is therefore a good one, and is also only secured on one person or at the most on one couple. It is easier to gauge the overall risk when only one or two people are involved than if several people are involved, as may be the case with, for example, a newly-formed company.

The risk that exists with a building society mortgage when it is originally made is reduced by the fact that the borrower is normally paying back capital with his interest payments, and the original sum lent is therefore decreasing with time. Allied to the decrease in the size of the loan, if there also happens to be an increase in house prices over a period, then the two factors operate together to increase the security of the loan. As the size of the loan decreases, the value of the property on which it is secured increases.

There are other sources of finance for residential house-purchase, but the majority of people do in fact borrow from building societies when buying a house. In recent years there has been a change of policy amongst the High Street banks regarding offering loans for house purchase. In the past United Kingdom banks were not active in this field, and such loans as they did make tended to be for relatively short terms and at higher rates of interest than those offered by building societies. However, several of the major banks have now entered the house mortgage market in direct competition with the building societies and are offering mortgages at very competitive terms in a similar way to banks in other countries. Private mortgages can also be obtained, that is, a mortage from one individual to another, the house-purchaser. These now tend to be few in number, possibly because there are few people with sufficient liquid capital to lend for such purposes, and because those who wish to lend on a private mortgage would be competing with the building society rate of interest, which would often be lower than that which they could obtain from alternative sources. Also, private lenders in most cases will wish to retain a degree of liquidity which might be unacceptable to the would-be borrower, who would not want to run the risk of having the borrowed money recalled at short notice. To negotiate a satisfactory private mortgage, the terms would have to be such as were acceptable to both the lender and the borrower.

When money is required for investment purposes or the purchase of commercial properties, the sum the borrower requires will probably be considerably larger than that which the average house-purchaser requires, since units of commercial property are generally much more valuable than the average house. The would-be investor or purchaser will usually have to have recourse to the commercial money market and the larger lending institutions for his funds. At times he may be able to obtain finance from the commercial banks, but such lending is likely to be for a short term only, and therefore likely to be relatively unattractive to a borrower unless he can be reasonably certain that the loan will be renewed at regular intervals, thereby making it in effect a long-term loan. Even if continued renewal gives in effect a long-term loan, it is probable that the rate of interest charged would vary with fluctuations in interest rates generally and such an arrangement might not be acceptable to a borrower, as he would be unable to predict the long-term viability of a project with any degree of certainty.

In many cases a purchaser of commercial investment property will borrow his money from a finance house, or a body such as one of the larger insurance companies. Insurance Companies do lend for such purposes, although in these days the majority of them probably prefer to invest directly in property.

The rate of interest charged on commercial loans will invariably be well in excess of that charged by building societies. The lender of money for commercial purposes has the objective of making money himself, and so the rate of interest charged will not only have to cover his own operating costs but also have to produce a profit. This will have to be sufficient to make up for any profit that could have been made had the money been used in other ways. This concept is commonly referred to by economists as the "opportunity cost" of money, and unless a lender can make as much profit out of a loan as he could have made in the next best alternative opportunity open to him, then he will be ill-advised to lend money for the purchase of commercial property. This comparison will dictate the lowest rate of interest at which a lender can offer his money, and over and above that he will also wish to obtain sufficient profit to cover any additional risk which the loan may entail. The alternative source of investment open to him may be less risky than lending on commercial property, and he would therefore be unwise to lend unless he received an extra payment to cover the extra risk.

In deciding what the opportunity cost of his money is, a lender will consider all the other investment opportunities open to him, and this will include the possibility of investing money in himself. Unless more money can be made by lending than could be made by using his savings in a business venture of his own, he is unlikely to lend. He is also likely to be influenced by the rate of interest offered by other people wishing to borrow money, and this may entail consideration of the international money market and the rates offered therein, also the rates offered nationally, such as those paid by local authorities and other public bodies who wish to obtain loans from individuals.

There is little doubt that lending for commercial purposes is normally riskier than the type of lending engaged in by building societies. The trouble experienced by fringe banks in the United Kingdom during 1974 illustrates how such risks may be rapidly increased by changing economic trends. The risk in commercial lending for property purchase revolves around a variety of other factors apart from the property. The use to which it is going to be put will be an important factor, and the riskier the use and the smaller the market for such uses, the less secure the loan is likely to be in the long term. If there is a great demand for property for a particular use and few properties are available, the risk is likely to be reduced. However, even if this is the case, there may be a rapid change if the general economic situation suddenly changes. Should there be a slump in the economy it may soon become apparent that a shortage of property has rapidly become a surplus as a result of potential property users disappearing from the market. Whereas this may happen in the commercial property market during bad times, people will still need houses in which to live, and so, in this respect, commercial property is probably a greater risk than owner-occupied residential property.

As with residential property, the character and ability of the user will also be very important. This may be quite difficult to assess if the purchaser is a company in which a number of individuals are combining in a joint enterprise. It may not even be certain that they have the ability to carry out the enterprise, or even the ability to get on together as people. As the board of directors of a company may change frequently and even rapidly, it may be even more difficult to assess the security to the lender if changes do occur in its constitution.

For these and other reasons the lender of money which is to be used for the purchase of commercial property will "vet" both the scheme and the borrower very carefully and endeavour to ensure that the rate of interest he receives on the loan is adequate to cover all the risks involved. As there is also invariably considerable competition for a limited supply of funds, the commercial money rate is again likely to be relatively high. Often there will be demands for more money than the total available to lend, and the supply and demand situation will in such cases result in lenders being able to demand a high rate of interest, which they will more often than not succeed in obtaining. As long as the borrower considers that the money he borrows will provide him with greater returns than the cost of borrowing, a loan at a high rate of interest will still be a viable proposition to him.

The term "gearing" refers to the relationship between the money an investor puts into a scheme himself, and the money he borrows for the scheme. The money which he provides himself is referred to as his "equity" in the scheme.

Where the equity is a small proportion of the total capital involved, and the greater part is money which has been borrowed, the project is referred to as being highly-geared, and where the converse is the case the project will be said to enjoy a low gearing. The degree of gearing has been an important factor in property investment since the second world war, and the rate of interest charged on borrowed money has also been important. A series of simple examples follows which it is hoped will illustrate the differences which result from varying degrees of gearing and from borrowing at varying rates of interest. It will be seen that there may be terrific, sometimes terrifying, implications to the investor resulting from increases or decreases in the rate of interest, and that this, combined with the degree of gearing, will be critical in determining the viability of an investment. The examples are purposely kept simple, and such items as tax relief on borrowed money are ignored; it is assumed that the cost of the money to the investor is the total cost after allowing for incidental costs and tax relief on the loans.

Example 1

A property which produces a net income of £10,000 per annum is purchased for £100,000 the investor providing all the purchase money himself.

Annual income net of outgoings   £10,000

$$\text{Yield to investor} = \frac{10,000}{100,000} \times 100 = \underline{\underline{10\%}}$$

Example 2
As example 1, but the investor borrows £50,000 of the purchase money at a rate of interest of 7%.

Annual income net of outgoings	£10,000
Deduct interest on loan of £50,000 @ 7%	3,500
Net income to investor	£ 6,500

$$\text{Yield on investor's equity} = \frac{6,500}{50,000} \times 100 = \underline{\underline{13\%}}$$

Example 3
As example 1, but the investor borrows £75,000 of the purchase money at a rate of interest of 7%.

Annual income net of outgoings	£10,000
Deduct Interest on loan of £75,000 @ 7%	5,250
Net income to investor	£ 4,750

$$\text{Yield on investor's equity} = \frac{4,750}{25,000} \times 100 = \underline{\underline{19\%}}$$

It can be seen from the above examples that if the cost of borrowing is below the overall yield on the total capital invested, an investor can increase the yield on his equity by increasing his gearing. The higher the gearing, the greater will be the yield on his equity, and the lower the gearing the smaller will be the yield on his equity. Whatever the gearing, as long as the cost of borrowing money remains below the overall yield on his property, the project will remain financially sound.

Example 4
As example 1, but the investor borrows £50,000 of the purchase money at a rate of interest of 15%.

Annual income net of outgoings	£10,000
Deduct Interest on loan of £50,000 @ 15%	7,500
Net income to investor	£ 2,500

$$\text{Yield on investor's equity} = \frac{2,500}{50,000} \times 100 = \underline{\underline{5\%}}$$

Example 5

As example 1, but the investor considers borrowing £75,000 of the purchase money at a rate of interest of 15%.

Annual Income net of outgoings	£10,000
Deduct Interest on loan of £75,000 @ 15%	11,250
Loss to investor	£ 1,250

The last two examples illustrate that although the cost of borrowing money is greater than the overall yield obtained from the property, the project remains financially profitable if the investor's gearing is low enough to provide a return on his money, even though that return is below the overall return to the property. In example 5 the investor is so highly geared that, after paying interest charges, there will be no return left to his equity. Indeed on the figures used in example 5 he would actually be out of pocket and it would be inadvisable for him to proceed with the venture.

Example 6 will investigate the break-even point and it will be shown that a point will be reached at which if the investor increases his borrowing an overall loss will be made. It is worth noting that, even in the type of situation illustrated in example 5, an investor may consider going ahead with the project if he takes the view that the income is likely to increase sufficiently at a relatively early date to enable it to become viable and to give him an adequate return to his equity.

Example 6

As example 1 with the cost of borrowing at 15%. The total interest paid cannot exceed £10,000 if the investor is not to make a loss. Let the maximum capital which can be borrowed = X

$$X \times \frac{15}{100} = 10,000 \qquad \frac{15X}{100} = 10,000 \qquad 15X = 1,000,000$$

$$X = £66,666.66$$

These are very simple examples which illustrate several different aspects of gearing and the importance of the rate of interest, but in reality it can be very difficult indeed accurately to predict the constituent parts of such calculations. It may be difficult to estimate the net income which will be obtained. If the property is not yet occupied by a tenant, and a tenant has to be found, it is a matter of opinion as to the rent which may be obtained. In the examples above if the actual rent obtained was £1,000 less or £1,000 more than that which was anticipated, completely different results would be obtained from the calculations. Again, it may be that the investor has to pay various outgoings from his gross income, and fluctuations in the cost of repairing and insuring a property may result in fluctuations in the net income obtained. As we are aware of the investor's liability to pay income-tax on the income-flow, it should be noted that fluctuations in the rate of income-tax or corporation tax will result not only in a variation in the income available for spending after tax has been paid, but in variations in the net cost to him of borrowing money, as if there is a decrease in the amount of tax payable the amount of tax relief obtained on the loan costs will also decrease, and so the true cost of borrowing will increase.

Occurrences such as those mentioned above will tend to upset the investor's original predictions and calculations. Indeed, possibly the most important of the variables discussed above is the actual rent obtainable, and although over the past twenty years or so rent levels have generally increased, this does not rule out the possibility of decreases in the future. Such an occurrence could follow either a change in the supply position of properties, or a change in demand resulting from economic trends generally. Whatever the reason for a change in any of the variables, if one does occur the yield on the investor's equity will be changed at the same time.

During 1974 many British property companies ran into considerable difficulties because of the general increase in the cost of borrowing money. This increase resulted in borrowing costs being considerably higher than they had been a year or two earlier, and in many cases the cost of borrowing even doubled. These increases automatically took some companies from a position such as that illustrated by examples 2 or 3 to the position illustrated in example 5. There were also other factors helping to cause the difficulties experienced by some companies, particularly a freeze on business rents which was introduced as one of a series of moves intended to arrest inflation in the economy generally. The combination of a freeze on rents which prevented higher rents being obtained even where legally they could otherwise have been collected, combined with an increase in the rate of interest payable on borrowed money, took many companies into a position in which they were losing considerable sums of money on investments. The higher the gearing of a company in such a situation, the greater the problems caused by an increase in interest rates. The reader may care to do a few calculations himself using progressively higher rates of interest and progressively higher degrees of gearing to illustrate the problems encountered by many companies.

If interest rates rise as they have done in recent years, the problems encountered by an investor can still be solved if the rate of interest he has to pay remains below the yield he obtains from the property, but the more the interest rate exceeds the yield from his investment, the greater the problem he will face. In more fortunate times for property developers, many made fortunes because they were able to borrow money at low rates of interest to invest in properties which produced a higher yield. It should not be forgotten that the developers who did this had great foresight, and that the majority of them also had considerable development skills which they utilised in their projects. They were also prepared to take what were considered great risks at the time, and even though, with the benefit of hindsight, we may consider their successful projects and say "Well they couldn't have lost", it should not be forgotten that at the time they ventured on them many people considered them very foolish and unwise.

The developers who made fortunes by borrowing at low interest rates were in fact borrowing on the basis illustrated in examples 2 and 3, and, because the interest charged was low in comparison with the yield from the property, they obtained high yields on their equity. The higher their gearing, the higher the yield they obtained on their equity. With time, the yield increased even more because incomes obtained from property investments increased almost dramatically following the general increase in rent levels which arose from the seemingly ever-increasing demand for commercial property during the post-war years.

Examples to illustrate the positions of two developers/investors following increases in the rent obtainable from their properties are given below.

Example 7

A property which produces a net income of £20,000 per annum was purchased for £200,000, the investor borrowing £100,000 of the purchase money at a rate of interest of 7%.

Annual income net of outgoings	£20,000
Deduct Interest on £100,000 @ 7%	7,000
Net income to investor	£13,000

$$\text{Yield on investor's equity} = \frac{13,000}{100,000} \times 100 = \underline{\underline{13\%}}$$

Example 8

As example 7 but the income has increased to £40,000 per annum.

Annual income net of outgoings	£40,000
Deduct Interest on £100,000 @ 7%	7,000
Net income to investor	£33,000

$$\text{Yield on investor's equity} = \frac{33,000}{100,000} \times 100 = \underline{\underline{33\%}}$$

Examples 7 and 8 illustrate the very considerable improvement in the investor's overall position, as, with a doubling in the income produced by the property, the yield on the equity has almost trebled. The reader may care to do calculations to work out what the yield on the investor's equity would be if the interest rate in each case doubles to 14%.

Example 9

A property which produces a net income of £20,000 per annum is purchased for £200,000, the investor borrowing £150,000 of the purchase money at a rate of interest of 7%.

Annual income net of outgoings	£20,000
Deduct Interest on £150,000 @ 7%	10,500
Net income to investor	£ 9,500

$$\text{Yield on investor's equity} = \frac{9,500}{50,000} \times 100 = \underline{\underline{19\%}}$$

It will be noted that by borrowing a larger sum of money at 7% the investor has increased the yield on his own money in comparison with the situation in example 7.

Example 10

As example 9, but the income has increased to £40,000 per annum.

Annual income net of outgoings	£40,000
Deduct Interest on £150,000 @ 7%	10,500
Net income to investor	£29,500

$$\text{Yield on investor's equity} = \frac{29,500}{50,000} \times 100 = \underline{\underline{59\%}}$$

These examples illustrate that high gearing can sometimes produce very profitable results, but it must be remembered that it can equally well be very, very risky. It is easy to be wise after the event, and it is too easy to comment that many developers and investors who encountered difficulties in 1974 were foolhardy and deserved all the problems they encountered. A generous person might comment that in more fortunate times, when the underlying factors of the market moved in their favour rather than against them, they might have been considered skilful and foresighted. However, the vagaries of the economy and the market are problems which an investor or developer has to accept, and one of the great skills needed in property investment is in estimating accurately the necessary financial requirement of a project, and thereafter borrowing on the right terms to obtain an acceptable yield on the equity and thereby to make a scheme viable. If, having made all these predictions and calculations, the investor is unable to borrow on the right terms, he would be ill-advised to proceed with a project.

As shown above, changes in circumstances can improve the investor's lot, but it should not be forgotten by those who might begrudge him high returns that such changes can also cause great problems and may result in considerable money losses being made, to say nothing of the mental strain and worry caused when adverse conditions arise.

CHAPTER 23

CONCLUSION

The valuation menu has been studied and it is hoped the reader considers he has also tasted an appetiser. If enough has been gleaned from this book to encourage further pursuit of the study of valuation, and if it has helped him or her to acquire a reasonable understanding of the topics covered in it, the author will consider it to have been well worth writing.

APPENDIX

VALUATION METHODS

RECONCILIATION OF VARIOUS INTERNATIONAL VALUATION METHODS

GREAT BRITAIN	AUSTRALIA	U.S.A.
COMPARATIVE METHOD	*DIRECT COMPARISON*	*MARKET DATA OR SALES COMPARISON*

The most widely used method of valuation entailing a valuation of property by direct comparison with similar properties that have been sold. This method is used where sale property and property to be valued are sufficiently similar to enable a value to be applied to the subject property on the strength of sales evidence.

CONTRACTORS' METHOD	*SUMMATION*	*COST OR SUMMATION APPROACH*

This method is employed in the absence of comparable sales or earning rates. Usually a last resort method which assumes a relationship between cost and value. *Equation:* Cost of site + cost of building − obsolescence − depreciation = value of property. (Used in valuation of Hospitals, Schools, Police Stations, etc., where no comparable sales exist.)

INVESTMENT METHOD	*CAPITALISATION*	*INCOME OR RESIDUAL EARNINGS APPROACH*

This method is used where there is a direct relationship between anticipated annual income and sale price for comparable properties sold and the property to be valued. Sales analysis will provide a factor or multiplier by which anticipated annual income is multiplied to give the capital value. Discounted cash flow techniques can be used.

In Great Britain and Australia the factor or multiplier is known as the "Years Purchase".

Income can be capitalised net or gross.

Capitalisation rate = Income expressed as a percentage of Capital Value.

Equation: Value = Income × year's purchase.

"Direct Capitalisation": Value
= Income × Factor.

"Yield Capitalisation": Future benefits converted to present value with a required profit rate.

"Residual" techniques. Here a component or part is known or can be estimated. Income for this part is deducted from total income leaving a residual income which is capitalised to give the value of the unknown portion. *"Building Residual"* technique is applied when land value is known. *"Land Residual"* technique is applied when building value is known.

RESIDUAL METHOD   *HYPOTHETICAL DEVELOPMENT*   *LAND DEVELOPMENT OF COST OF LAND*

PRODUCTION APPROACH

This valuation approach is employed for property with development or redevelopment potential. *Equation:* Value of completed development – total expenditure (including developer's profit) = Present value of land. D.C.F. Techniques can be employed.

PROFITS (or "ACCOUNTS") METHOD
Used where there are no comparable sales and there is some degree of monopoly either legal (licenced, etc.) or factual.

Equation: **GROSS EARNINGS**

       Less **PURCHASES**

       = **GROSS PROFIT**

       Less **WORKING EXPENSES**
           (except rent)

       = **NET PROFIT**

Rental value determined from net profit.
This method used for hotels, cinemas, etc.

PRODUCTIVE UNIT

The market may provide an indication that buyers will pay a price for certain units, i.e. the sale of orchards may indicate a certain price per tree plus structural improvements; with rural land "Sheep Area" values are produced by the market.

INDEX